AF624060

Discrimination Against Women In India (A Gender Study)

Discrimination Against Women In India (A Gender Study)

By

Justice Raj Kumar Manisana Singh

AKANSHA PUBLISHING HOUSE
NEW DELHI-110002 (INDIA)

AKANSHA PUBLISHING HOUSE
4649-B/21, Ansari Road
Darya Ganj, New Delhi - 110 002
Ph.: 23263193 / 9811582579 / 09435116718
Fax: 011-23263193
Email: ektabooks@yahoo.com

Discrimination Against Women in India: A Gender Study

© Author

First Published 2008
ISBN–978–81–8370–148-8

All rights reserved. No part of this publication may be reproduced or transmitted, in any form or by any means, without prior permission of the author. Any person who does any unauthorized act in relation to this publication may be liable to criminal prosecution and civil claims for damages.

[The responsibility for the facts stated, conclusions reached etc., is entirely that of the author. The publisher is not responsible for them, whatsoever.]

PRINTED IN INDIA

Published by Akansha Publishing House, New Delhi and Printed at Aryan Enterprises, Delhi.

Dedicated
To
Women of India

CONTENTS

CONTENTS

PREFACE

When I was a Judge, I had to deal with varieties of cases of violation of Constitutional rights of women and therefore had to study the relevant laws on the subject and the judicial pronounce-ments (if any) by making a research. In the matter of rape cases, the award of compensation to the victim is of a recent origin after the Supreme Court's decisions holding that the case of rape is not only a criminal offence, it also violative of human rights provided under Article 21 of the Constitution, namely Right to Life.

When I was the Chairperson of the Assam Human Rights Commission, I had to face violation of human rights of women such as custodial rape, violation of privacy of women, etc. A mention may be made here that the procedure to be followed in disposing of the cases before the Commission is prescribed under the Protection of Human Rights Act, as distinct from the procedure followed in the court of law.

I have been participating in seminars and conferences relating to gender justice. I, therefore, have to make preparation for seminars or conferences by reading various literatures and International Instruments relating to gender equality.

My study of women related-laws and literatures shows Women, in general, are placed in a very disadvantageous position; women are treated as third-class citizens and are subservient to the social, economic and political order; and women have been victims of violence and exploitation at every stage of life but the women continue to endure the oppression. Although women cannot be equal to men in all the spheres of life and in all situations because of marked or natural biological deference, men and women must have at least equal rights to enjoy the fundamental freedoms and human rights, particularly in political, economic, social, cultural and civil situations — hence this book.

Rajkumar Manisana Singh

1

GENDER INJUSTICE

Men's Oppression

Everywhere in the world of today, people are voicing about the protection of human rights and fundamental freedoms of women. The question is : Why or how does such a question arise in this modern world and advanced society.

In the history of patriarchal society in India, one of the most important part of it is a variety of discriminations against women, including cruelty to women and men's oppression of women. Some of the instances are— Hindu women had no right to own property as full owners before the Hindu Succession Act 1956; inequality of reward for equal work; repeated demand of dowry and killing of brides by burning or otherwise; sexual abuse and sexual harassment and so on. In other words, women, in general, are placed in a very disadvantageous position; women are treated as third- class citizens and remain subservient to the social, economic and political order; and women had been victims of violence and exploitation at every stage of life but the women continue to endure the oppression.

Women oppression starts from womb to grave; and some of prominent facts are—

In womb	-	Abortion or foeticide in preference for male babies.
As a baby	-	Female infanticide, scolding, discrimination in medical attention and food.
As a child	-	Child marriage, sexual abuse, child prostitution, incest.
As girl	-	Sexual abuse, financial exploitation, violence at work place, sex exploitation, forced prostitution, abduction.
As a wife	-	Cheating by husband and family members, violence, dowry murder, psychological violence, sex violence at work spot and elsewhere.
At the old age	-	Discrimination against widows, economical disadvantage, slander.

Although there is marked or natural biological difference between men and women, their basic requirements for human existence are the same such as food requirements, clothing requirements, housing requirements, and such other things required for their livelihood. In spite of these facts, there is gender bias against women for whatever the reason may be. One of the reasons for gender injustice against women may be the harmful customs and usages or practices prevailing for centuries prescribing **moral code of conducts**, as distinct from legal rights and obligations, namely **what women should do or should not do**.

Social Status of Women

Women have been socially, economically, psychologically, physically and sexually exploited sometimes in the name of religion, sometimes on the pretext of writing scriptures, sometime by social sanction etc. Women are considered in the family as dependent; they face restriction on their movement opportunities, which affect their education, economic opportunities etc. Women and girls are often kept at home to help the families, and are responsible for household needs. And they are fed last, resulting in a diet of low in calories and proteins. Women are regarded as expendable assets. There is a large segment of society which have traditionally been subjected to unjust treatment; women are one of such segment; and women are backward in education and political participation. In other words, women are backward class as compared to men.

Constitutional Provisions

The founding fathers of the Constitution of India were very much aware of the history of mankind about the gender injustice, i.e. they were aware of historic injustices and inequities towards women. They realised that injustices and inequities could be redressed by the constitutional means. Therefore, the principle of gender equality has been enshrined in the Constitution of India (which came into force on 26 January 1950) in its Preamble and Chapters on "Fundamental Rights", "Fundamental Duties" and "Directive Principles of State Policy". The Constitution not only grants equality to women, but also empowers the State to make special laws for protecting women from discrimination. The Constitution has, now, provided reservation of seats for women in Municipalities and Panchayats, after amending the Constitution in 1993.

Women-related Laws

Having regard to the changing social realities and emerging trends in the nature of crime, the Government of India has been reviewing the existing laws and system of administration of justice with a view to devising effective and efficient methods of dealing with the women-related situations. The Government has, after the commencement of the Constitution, enacted a number of woman-related laws for the purpose of removing gender bias and for the promotion and protection of women's human rights. Some of them are the Dowry Prohibition Act of 1961, the Equal Remuneration Act of 1976, the Maternity Benefit Act of 1961, the Indecent Representation of Women (Prohibition) Act of 1986, the Commission of Sati (Prohibition) Act of 1987, the National Commission for Women Act of 1990, the Pre-Natal Diagnostic Techniques (Regulation and Prevention of Misuse) Act of 1994 and the Protection of Women from Domestic Violence Act of 2005 etc; and the procedural laws, Evidence Act, CrPC and other women-related procedural laws, have been amended.

The International Community is also much concerned about the equal rights of men and women to enjoy all the economic, social, cultural, civil and political rights. Therefore, the Universal Declaration of Human Rights was adopted by the General Assembly of the United Nations on 10 December 1948. Later the 10th of December, come to be known as **"The Human Right Day"** is celebrated on the 10th December of every year. Everyone is entitled to all the rights and freedoms set forth in the Declaration, without distinction of any kind, such as race, colour, **sex**, language, religion, political or other opinion, national or social origin, property, birth or other status.

India has also endorsed or ratified the following women-related International instruments, namely— The Mexico Plan of Action (1975), the Nairobi Forward-Looking Strategies (1985), the Beijing Declaration and (the) Platform for Action (1995) and the Convention on the Elimination of All Forms of Discrimination against Women (1979). The "Further actions and initiatives to implement the Beijing Declaration and the Platform for Action" has also been endorsed by India for appropriate follow-up. Thereafter, the National Policy for the Empowerment of Women 2001 was brought out by the Government of India in view of the provisions prescribed in the "Further actions and initiatives to implement the

Beijing Declaration and the Platform for Action" under the caption "Actions to be taken at the national level".

Effect of Existing Laws

The complaint of the people is that it is not the absence of law, but the lack of the implementation of laws, which results in the failure to protect the gender inequality. Despite plethora of laws the status of women is not better than ever. So many social changes have been made; the bias of caste and creed had more or less disappeared; but the gender bias is not. However, there are innumerable instances where women are worshipped in different forms— may be in special cases.

Today, in comparison with men, there are many women who are successful doctors, engineers, teachers, planners, managers, politicians and pilots, who have encountered their harmful family and community traditions and practices, but the conservatism by its harmful Moral Code of Conducts limits women's freedom to enjoy their rights guaranteed by the Constitution and other relevant laws. Despite the religious sanction and conservative views, women of high-status or educated mothers are in a different footing.

2

JUDICIAL RESPONSE TO GENDER JUSTICE

Judicial Pronouncements

The Supreme Court has responded gender justice (gender issue) in favour of women considering the provisions of gender equality guaranteed by the Constitution of India as well as International Instruments to which India is one of the States Parties or to which India had acceded or ratified. Some of the judicial pronouncements are described below.

In **Miss CB Muthamma vs Union of India,** AIR 1979 SC 1868, the Supreme Court has declared that the service rules of the Indian Foreign Service requiring a female employee to obtain permission of the Government in writing before her marriage and denial of right to employment to a married woman are ultra vires as the rules are discriminatory against women. The Supreme Court has, however, remarked that the equality of opportunity in matters relating to employment does not, however, mean that men and women are equal in all occupations and in all situations.

The Supreme Court has, in **Air India vs Nergesh Meerza**, AIR 1981 SC 1828, declared that the rule providing pregnancy a bar to continue in service of an Air Hostess is ultra vires of the Constitution.

In **Shobha Rani vs Madhukar Reddi,** AIR 1988 SC 121: (1988)1SCC 105, the Supreme Court has held that the repeated demand of dowry amounts to cruelty under the Hindu Marriage Act.

In **Bodhisttwa Gautam vs Subhra Chakraborty,** AIR 1996 SC 922: (1996)1 SCC 490, the Supreme Court has held that rape is not only an offence in criminal law, it is also violative of human rights, namely Right to Life contained in Article 21 of the Constitution. The Supreme Court has also held that fundamental rights can be enforced even against the private bodies and individuals.

In **Nilabati Behera Vs State of Orissa,** (1993)2SCC 746, the Supreme Court considered provisions in the ICCPR (International Covenant on Civil and Political Rights) in order to support the view that "an enforceable right to compensation is not alien to the concept of enforcement of a guaranteed rights" as a public law remedy under Article 32, distinct from the private law remedy in torts. In Nilabati's case compensation awarded to the next of the kin of deceased.

In **Githa Hariharan Vs Reserve Bank of India,**(1999)2SCC 228: AIR 1999 SC 1149, the Supreme Court has, after considering the Universal Declaration of Human Rights, Convention on the

Elimination of All Forms of Discrimination against Women (1979) and the Beijing Declaration on Status of Women, held that mother and father are of the same status as guardian of a minor under the Hindu Minority and Guardianship Act, 1956.

In **Chairman, Railway Board vs Mrs Chandrima Das,** AIR 2000 SC 988, the Supreme Court has affirmed award of compensation of Rs.ten lakhs to Bangladeshi woman, who was a victim of gang rape committed by the railway employees in the railway building, by holding that foreign national can be granted relief under public law for violation of fundamental rights. The Supreme Court also has observed that International Covenants and Declarations as adopted by the United Nations are to be respected by all signatories.

In **Municipal Corporation of Delhi vs Female Workers** (Muster Roll), AIR 2000 SC 1274, the benefits under the Maternity Benefit Act was made available to a class of the Delhi Corporation. However, those benefits were denied to the women employees engaged on muster-roll on the ground that they were not regular employees. The Supreme Court has, after considering the provision under the Convention on the Elimination of All Forms of Discrimination against Women, held that the benefits under the Maternity Benefit Act cannot be denied to Muster-roll employees.

The Supreme Court has also observed that clause (3) of Article 15 of the Constitution, which permits special provision for women and children, has been widely resorted to and the Supreme Court has upheld that the validity of special measures in legislation or executive orders favouring women (see **Yusuf vs State of Bombay,** AIR 1954SC 321, **State of AP vs PB Vijoy Kumar**, AIR 1995 SC 1648 and **Union of India vs KP Prabhakaram,** (1997) 11SC 638. The Supreme Court has also given sufficient sustenance to reservation in services for backward classes; and women as a class are backward (see **Indira Sawhney vs Union of India**, AIR 1993 SC 477, a nine- judge bench).

Law Declared by the Supreme Court

At this stage, a decision of the Supreme Court reported as **Vishaka vs State of Rajasthan**, AIR 1997 SC 3011 : (1997)6 SCC 241, may be referred to. In that case, there was brutal gang rape of a social worker in a village of Rajasthan. In the context of sexual feelings, the Supreme Court defined "sexual harassment" and formulated "preventive steps" to prevent sexual harassment in the exercise of the power available under Article 32 of the Constitution for the enforcement of the fundamental rights; the Court also said that the definition of "sexual harassment" and the formulation of "preventive steps" would be treated as the law declared by the Supreme Court under Article 141 of the Constitution as there was no specific law in that regard.

The definition of "sexual harassment" is as under–

"For this purpose, sexual harassment includes such unwelcome sexually determined behaviour (whether directly or by implication) as :

(a) physical contact and advances;

(b) a demand or request for sexual favours;

(c) sexually-coloured remarks;

(d) showing pornography;

(e) any other unwelcome physical, verbal or non-verbal conduct of sexual nature".

Preventive steps :

"All employers or persons in charge of workplace whether in the public or private sector should take appropriate steps to prevent sexual harassment. Without prejudice to the generality of this obligation they should take the following steps:

(a) Express prohibition of sexual harassment as defined above at the work place should be notified, published and circulated in appropriate ways.

(b) The rules/regulations of the government and public sector bodies relating to conduct and discipline should include rules/regulations prohibiting sexual harassment and provide for appropriate penalties in such rules against the offender;

(c) As regards private employers steps should be taken to include the aforesaid prohibitions in the standing orders under the Industrial Employment (Standing Orders) Act, 1946.

(d) Appropriate work conditions should be provided in respect of work, leisure, health and hygiene to further ensure that there is no hostile environment towards women at workplaces and no woman employee should have reasonable grounds to believe that she is disadvantaged in connection with her employment".

Reliance to International Instruments

From the above, it appears that the Supreme Court has frequently relied upon the Universal Declaration of Human Rights (1948), the International Covenant on Civil and Political Rights (1966), the International Covenant on Economic, Social and Cultural Rights (1966), the Convention on the Elimination of All Forms of Discrimination against Women (1979) and the Beijing Declaration and the Platform for Action (1995). In other words, the Supreme Court has been so much influenced by the women's rights embodied in the above Declarations, Covenants and Conventions while construing domestic laws. The Article 253 of the Constitution confers exclusive power on the Parliament for legislation for implementing any treaty, agreement or convention with any other country or countries or any decision made at any international conference, association or other body. But, in the absence of such legislations, the Supreme Court views that the Courts are under an obligation to give due regard to the International Conventions and norms for construing domestic laws, more so, when there is no in consistency between them (International instruments and domestic laws) and there is a void in domestic laws (see **Apparel Export Promotion Council vs AK Chopra**, (1999)1 SCC 754: AIR 1999 SC 625, **Gramophone Company of India Ltd. Vs BB Pandey**, AIR 1984 SC 667 and **Vineet Narain vs Union of India**, 1998 SC 889).

A mention may be made that in Nilabati's case (supra), the Supreme Court observed: "There is no reason why these international conventions and norms cannot, therefore, be used for construing the fundamental rights expressly guaranteed in the Constitution of India which embody the basic concept of gender equality in all sphere of human activity".

3

HUMAN RIGHTS AND PROTECTION OF HUMAN RIGHTS

Human Rights

Rights of man are not the only rights those created by man such as laws made by the legislators (legislative body), customs and usages having the force of law; beyond those rights created by man, there lies another idea or concept of rights of man, otherwise known as the "natural rights" originated from the nature (say, Law of Nature), that is to say, those rights originated from nature (under the law of nature) are called the "natural rights", for example – natural right to the flow of light and air, natural right to the purity of air, natural rights in water of stream or river etc. Those natural rights are nothing but human rights. Therefore, human rights are natural rights spring from human itself and are the rights which are inherent in human beings. Some call the human rights as the " birth rights". They are not acquired, nor transferred nor extinguished. Therefore, human rights differs from those man made rights, which can be extinguished or acquired or transferred, as the case may be.

Out of the natural rights or human rights, those which are fundamental or principal rights (for instance – right to life, liberty, equality and dignity of individual) are commonly called as the "basic human rights" or "fundamental human rights". But what are the basic human rights cannot be listed exhaustively till date.

International Protection of Human Rights

It has a long history. There has been a growing concern about the protection of human rights, but the rules and machinery for the International Legal Protection of the Rights and Freedoms of the individual are in large measure a post-1945 development (after the end of World War II).

There were several International and regional instruments for the protection of human rights. In other words, as a subject of practical importance in terms or use of the protection of the equality and dignity of life of individual, it has become of greatly increased significance since the end of the World War II, for instance – European Convention on Human Rights. The impact of the Convention was that individuals could pursue rights outside the domestic court of their own state by taking complaints to the European Commission of Human Rights.

Post-1945 developments have produced a substantial number of treaty instruments. The Universal Declaration of Human Rights was adopted by the General Assembly of the United Nations on 10 December 1948 (see Appendix-I); and the 10th

December is known as the "Human Rights Day". It was mainly for the purpose of the International Protection of Human Rights. However, it was not a legally binding instrument, for the international community has no legislative body (Legislature). That apart, the rights included therein have only limited legal substance in the International Law. In that view of the matter, the Universal Declaration of Human Rights has been followed by several International Conventions and Covenants of which most significant are —

1. the International Covenant on Economic, Social and Cultural Rights; and
2. the International Covenant on Civil and Political Rights.

They were adopted by the General Assembly on 16 December 1966, and India is a party to the two Covenants.

None of the International Instruments specifically specifies/specify or lists/list what is/are the human rights which is/are to be protected or is/are intended to be protected. In spite of that the basic human rights to be protected are rights to life, liberty, equality and dignity of the individual. Other rights such as social and economic rights, etc are not clearly established. It may be stated that human rights and the protection of the human rights have been gradually growing up or developing because of the changing society, and the following human rights are, now, recognized or specified as the fundamental or basic human rights for protection, preservation and promotion —

1. Right to life,
2. Equality before law,
3. Freedom from torture, inhuman or degrading treatment or punishment,
4. Freedom from slavery and servitude,
5. Right to liberty and security of a person,
6. Right to fair and speedy trial,
7. Right to private and family life, or right to privacy.
8. Freedom of thoughts, conscience and religion,
9. Right to marry and find a family,
10. Freedom of expression,
11. Right of assembly & association,
12. Freedom of movement,
13. Right to property,
14. Right to education,
15. Right to free elections,
16. Right to economic and social provision; and
17. Collective Human Right (right of self-determination etc).

The list of rights and liberties is not a closed one. It cannot be so because of the changing social realities and emerging trends in nature of crime and violence.

Domestic Level Protection of Human Rights

Almost all the States (Countries) with written

Constitution have embodied some protection of the principal rights and liberties in their Constitutions within the framework of the Constitution.

As for India, the Fundamental Rights contained in Part III of the Constitution represent basic human rights possessed by every human body. Language recorded in Part III of the Constitution shows that it is the duty of, or an obligation imposed on, the State and its public functionaries (instrumentalities & agencies) to promote, protect and preserve human rights, as well as duty to prevent violation of human rights. However, the Supreme Court has held that fundamental rights can be enforced against the private bodies and individuals under Article 32 of the Constitution in view of public law remedy, distinct from private law remedy in tort [see Bodhisttwa Gautam's case (supra)].

Now, coming to the constitutional provision relating to the protection of Basic Human Rights or Fundamental Rights, the Constitution stipulates the enforcement of the Fundamental Rights when there is violation of basic human rights or fundamental rights or when there is an apprehension of violation of Fundamental Rights by the Supreme Court of India or the High Courts in India.

In addition to the Constitutional provisions for protection of human rights, the Protection of Human Rights Act of 1993 was enacted for, although India is a party to the International Covenants on Civil and Political Rights and the International Covenant on Economic, Social and Cultural Rights adopted by the

General Assembly of the United Nations on the 16th of December 1986 and the human rights embodied in the aforesaid Covenants stand substantially protected by the Constitution, there has been growing concern in the country and abroad about the issues of human rights and wide-ranging discussions were held at various fora such as Chief Ministers Conference on Human Rights, seminars organized in various parts of the country and meetings with leaders of various political parties.

Taking into account the views expressed in those discussions and having regard to the growing concern in the country and abroad, changing social realities and the emerging trends in the nature of crime and violence, the Human Rights Act of 1993 was enacted for the better protection of human rights and for matters connected therewith or incidental thereto.

Protection of Human Rights Act

Under the Human Rights Act of 1993, the National Human Rights Commission has been constituted, and some States of India have also constituted State Human Rights Commissions. The functions and powers of the National Human Rights Commission and the State Human Rights Commissions have been prescribed in the Human Rights Act. One of the main functions is to enquire into the complaint of violation of human rights or abetment thereof, or negligence in the prevention of such violation, by a public servant. There is also provision in the Human Rights Act for the establishment Human Rights Courts for the purpose of providing speedy trial of offences arising out of violation of human rights. The National Human Rights Commission, the State Human Rights Commissions and the human rights Courts are additional fora for better protection of human rights in addition to the Supreme Court and the High Courts.

Under the Human Rights Act, "human rights" means the rights relating to life, liberty, equality and dignity of the individual guaranteed by the Constitution or embodied in the International Covenants and enforceable by the Courts in India. Out of a number of existing basic human rights or fundamental rights, only a limited number of rights have been provided in the Human Rights Act, namely the rights relating to life, liberty, equality and dignity of the individual guaranteed by the Constitution or embodied in the International Covenants and enforceable by the Courts in India.

As regards the rights guaranteed by the Constitution, "rights to life and liberty" provided in the Human Rights Act are referable to Article 21 of the Constitution, which provides for "protection of life and liberties"; and that "right to dignity of the individual" (right to live with human dignity) flows from Article 21. The "right to equality" stipulated in the Human Rights Act is relatable to Article 14 of the Constitution which states "equality before law". Therefore, in view of the use of the expression "guaranteed by the Constitution", only those Fundamental Rights or Basic Human Rights guaranteed by the Constitution under Articles 14 and 21 are provided in the Human Rights Act, and not all the Fundamental Rights guaranteed by the Constitution.

In respect of the "International Covenants" mentioned in the Human Rights Act, "International Covenants" means the International Covenant on Civil and Political Rights and the International Covenant on Economic, Social and Cultural Rights adopted by the General Assembly of the United Nations on 16th December, 1986. As stated, India is a party to the two International Covenants. On a reading of the two International Covenants together with the Constitution, it appears that those human rights embodied in the two International Covenants are substantially protected by the Constitution. However, whether or not those fundamental human rights stipulated in the two International Covenants other than those protected by the Constitution can be enforced by the Courts in India cannot be put in a strait-jacket, it will depend upon the facts of each case considering the jurisdiction of the Supreme Court, the High Courts, the Human Rights Commissions and the Human Rights Courts.

Development of Human Rights

Human rights and the protection of human rights have gradually developed and are developing in India. In the development process, the Court has taken an important role, for example – the horizon of the "right to life" and "personal liberty" guaranteed by the Constitution under Article 21 has been expanded in different directions by the judicial pronouncements to the extent undreamed of by the founding fathers of the Constitution, or by the judges who gave it initial gloss; and, today, "right to life" guaranteed by the Constitution means something more than the survival of animal existence; it will include all those aspects of life, which go to make a man's life meaningful, complete, and worth living.

It may be stated that it was once thought that judges do not make laws; they only interpret. But, at present, this notion has been discarded everywhere. Every new decision on every new situation is development of law. Law is not static nor does it stand still. It moves continually to keep pace with the changing society. Where the law of the past does not fit in the present context, the Court evolves a new law. Law is growing to satisfy the need of the fast changing society. Therefore, "law" is a social machinery; and as a social machinery the law requires to remove any imbalance and to further progress serving all the needs of the Socialist Secular Democratic Republic under the rule of law. Considering this situation along with the provisions of the Directive Principles of State Policy enumerated under Part IV of the Constitution, the horizon of the "right to life" has been expanding.

About the Directive Principles of State Policy, the principles therein laid down are nevertheless fundamental in the governance of the country and it shall be the duty of the State to apply these principles in making laws. The opportunities and facilities provided under the Chapter on Directive Principles should be provided to the people. This being the situation, the Directive Principles are the Commands of or under the Constitution to the Legislature and Executive. Following the Commands, a large number of social legislations, rules and orders have been made by the competent authority for the welfare of the people in India; for instance – rights to rest and leisure by reduction of working day or hour, annual vacation with full pay for workers and employees, maternity and paternity leave, etc. That apart, the Directive Principles are taken into consideration in giving effect to the fundamental rights. To illustrate it, the right to live with human dignity derives its breadth from Directive Principles of State Policy. Therefore, Directive Principles have been elevated to Inalienable Fundamental Human Rights.

It may further be stated that Chapters on Fundamental Rights and Directive Principles of State Policy under the Constitution are integral part of the Constitution, but the Fundamental Rights guaranteed by the Constitution can be enforced in the Court of Law, whereas the Directive Principles cannot be enforced in the Court of Law as the Constitution itself prohibits the enforcement of the provisions of the Directive Principles (see Article 37). However, it does not mean that Directive Principles are less important than, or less inferior to, the Fundamental Rights; for the directive principles are Inalienable Fundamental Human Rights, as stated.

It has been stated that the horizon of the "right to life" has been expanded by the judicial pronouncements. At the present time, "right to life" includes the following rights – (1) right to live with human dignity; (2) right to education; (3) right against cruelty, physical or mental violence; (4) right to health; (5) right to healthy environment (which includes right to pollution free air, right to potable water and protection against hazardous industries); (6) right to access to road; (7) right to reasonable accommodation (right to shelter); (8) right to privacy; (9) right to livelihood (as distinguished from right to work); (10) Right to access to road; (11) right to immediate aid to starvation death; (12) right to removal of stench and stink caused by open drain and public excretion, and host of other rights. But the "right to die" and "right to work" are not included within the meaning of "right to life". However, "right to work" can be claimed after employment under Article 21.

This is how the human rights and protection of human rights have been developing in India. It would further develop more because of the changing social realities and emerging trends in nature of crime and violence.

4

CONVENTION ON THE ELIMINATION OF ALL FORMS OF DISCRIMINATION AGAINST WOMEN

Introduction

India has acceded to or ratified various International Conventions, Covenants and Human Rights instruments to secure the right of women. One of them is the ratification of the "Convention on the Elimination of All Forms of Discrimination against Women (1979)", otherwise known as the "CEDAW", in 1993. The Courts in India has referred to the CEDAW and relied on, even though there is no legislation made under Article 253 of the Constitution, as stated. It is believed that the CEDAW is one of the most powerful instruments for gender justice.

In Article 1 of the CEDAW, the expression "discrimination against women" has been defined thus–

"For the purposes of the present Convention, the term "discrimination against women" shall mean any distinction, exclusion or restriction made on the basis of sex which has the effect or purpose of impairing or nullifying the recognition, enjoyment or exercise by women, irrespective of their marital status, on a basis of equality of men and women, of human rights and fundamental freedom in the political, economic, social, cultural, civil or any other field".

In the above definition, the expression "human rights and fundamental freedom in political, economic, social, culture, civil or any other fields" has been emphasized. The term **"any other field"** is a very wide one, and this term shows that women and men are not equal in all spheres of human activities and in all situations. However, in the fields where women and men are to be treated as equal, this term **"any other field"** shall be applicable because of the use of the expression "All Forms of Discrimination" in the CEDAW. Be that as it may, States Parties in the Convention (CEDAW) condemned discrimination against women in all forms, and agreed to pursue by appropriate means and without delay a policy for elimination of discrimination against women; and for that purpose, States Parties undertook to legislate and also to take all appropriate measures enumerated in the CEDAW on the basis of equality of men and women.

Legislation Proposed to be made by the States Parties

In the above view of the matter, the States Parties, including India after ratifying the CEDAW, had undertaken to legislate against discrimination, among other things,—

a) To embody the principle of the equality of men and women in their national constitutions or other appropriate legislation if not yet incorporated therein and to ensure, through law, the practical realisation of this principle [see Article 2(a)].

b) To adopt appropriate legislative measures prohibiting all discrimination against women [see Article 2(b)].

c) To modify or abolish existing laws, regulations, customs and practices which constitute discrimination against women, if the other measures are not sufficient [see Article 2(f)].

d) To repeal all national penal provisions which constitute discrimination against women [see Article 2(g)].

e) To ensure the full development and advancement of women guaranteeing them the exercise and enjoyment of human rights and fundamental freedom on a basis of equality with men, in particular in the political, social, economic and cultural fields, if the other means are not sufficient (see Article 3).

f) To suppress all forms of traffic in women and exploitation of prostitution of women, if the other appropriate measures are not sufficient (see Article 6).

g) To specify a minimum age for marriage and to make the registration of marriage in an official registry compulsory [see Article 16(2)].

Measures Proposed to be taken by the States Parties

As regards the appropriate measures to be taken by the States Parties, some of them are—

a) To establish legal protection of the rights of women on an equal basis with men and to ensure through competent national tribunals and other public institutions the effective protection of women against any act of discrimination [see Article 2(c)].

b) To refrain from engaging in any act or practice of discrimination against women and to ensure the public authorities and institutions shall act in conformity with this obligation [see Article 2(d))]

c) To take all appropriate measures to eliminate discrimination against women by any person, organization or enterprise [see Article 2(e)].

d) To modify the social and cultural patterns of conduct of men and women, with a view to achieving the elimination of prejudices and customary and all other practices which are based on the idea of the inferiority or the superiority of either of the sexes or on stereotyped roles for men and women [see Article 5(a)].

e) To eliminate discrimination against women in the political and public life of the country and shall ensure to women, on equal terms with men , the rights, among other things,—

1) To participate in the formulation of government policy and the implementation thereof to hold public office and perform all public functions at all levels of government.
2) To participate in non-government organization and associations concerned with the public and political life of the country (see Article 7).

f) To ensure to women to represent their governments at the international level and to participate in the work of international organizations (see Article 8).

g) To grant women equal rights with men to acquire, change or retain their nationality [(see Article 9(1)].

h) To grant women equal rights with men with respect to the nationality of their children [(see Article 9(2)].

i) To ensure to women equal rights with men in the field of education, as well as, inter alia,

   1) The reduction of female student drop-out rates and the organization of programmes for girls and women who have left school prematurely.
   2) The opportunities to participate actively in sports and physical education.
   3) Access to specific educational information to help to ensure the health and well-being of families, including information and advice on family planning (see Article 10).

j) To eliminate discrimination against women in the field of employment in order to ensure, on a basis of equality of men and women, the same rights, among other things,—

1) the right to free choice of profession and employment, the right to promotion, job security and all benefits and conditions of service and the right to receive vocational training and retraining, including apprenticeship, advanced vocational training and recurrent training;

2) the right to equal remuneration, including benefits, and to equal treatment in respect of work of equal value, as well as equality of treatment in the evaluation of the quality of work;

3) the right to social security, particularly in cases of retirement, unemployment, sickness, invalidity and old age and other incapacity to work, as well as the right to paid leave;

4) the right to protection of health and to safety in working conditions, including the safeguarding of the function of reproduction;

5) to prohibit, subject to the imposition of sanctions, dismissal on the grounds of pregnancy or of maternity leave and discrimination in dismissals on the basis of marital status;

6) to provide special protection to women

during pregnancy in types of work proved to be harmful to them; and

7) to review periodically the legislation relating to matters of employment in the light of scientific and technological knowledge and shall be revised, repealed or extended as necessary (see Article 11).

k) To eliminate discrimination against women in the field of health care in order to ensure, on a basis of equality of men and women, access to health care services, including those related to family planning [see Article 12(1)].

l) To ensure to women appropriate services in connection with pregnancy, confinement and the post-natal period, granting free services where necessary, as well as adequate nutrition during pregnancy and lactation [see Article 12(2)].

m) To eliminate discrimination against women in other areas of economic and social life in order to ensure, on a basis of equality of men and women, the same rights, among other things,—

1) the right to bank loans, mortgages and other forms of financial credit; and

2) the right to participate in recreational activities, sports and all aspects of cultural life (see Article 13).

n) To take into account the particular problems faced by rural women and the significant roles which rural women play in the economic survival of their families, including their work in the non-monetized sectors of the economy, and shall take all appropriate measure to ensure the application of the provisions of this Convention (CEDAW) to women in rural areas [see Article 14(1)].

o) To eliminate discrimination against women in rural areas in order to ensure, on a basis of equality of men and women, that they participate in and benefit from rural development and shall ensure to such women the rights, among other things, —

1) to have access to adequate health cares facilities, including information, counseling and services in family planning;
2) to benefit directly from social security programmes;
3) to obtain all types of training and education, formal and non-formal, including that relating to functional literacy, as well as, inter alias, the benefit of all community and extension services, in order to increase their technical proficiency;
4) to organize self-help groups and co-operatives in order to obtain equal access to economic opportunities through employment or self employment;
5) to have access to agricultural credit and loans, marketing facilities, appropriate technology and equal treatment in land and agrarian reform as well as in land resettlement schemes; and

6) to enjoy adequate living conditions, particularly in relation to housing, sanitation, electricity and water supply, transport and communications [see Article 14(2)].

p) To accord to women equality with men before law (see Article 15).

q) To eliminate discrimination against women in all matters relating to marriage and family relations and shall ensure, on a basis of equality of men and women, inter alia, that—

1) the same rights and responsibilities with regard to guardianship, wardship, trusteeship and adoption of children, or similar institutions where these concepts exist in national legislation, in all cases the interests of the children shall be paramount; and

2) the same rights for both spouses in respect of the ownership, acquisition, management, administration, enjoyment and disposition of property, whether free of charge or for a valuable consideration (see Article 16).

Text of the CEDAW

As stated, the above are some of the measures to be taken by the States Parties, which appear to be prima facie relevant in the Indian context . The details of the CEDAW are described in Appendix –II of this book.

5

WORLD CONFERENCES ON STATUS OF WOMEN

The First World Conference on Women (Mexico Plan of Action – 1975)

The first world conference on status of women, otherwise known as the "Mexico Plan of Action", was held in Mexico in 1975 to coincide with 1975 International Women's Year. It was for the purpose of reminding the International Community that the discrimination against women continued to be a persistent problem in much of the world. The conference was called for by the United Nations General Assembly to focus, inter alia, plans of action for the advancement of women. For this purpose, the General Assembly identified three key objectives which would be the basis for the work of the United Nations on behalf of women, namely –

1. Full gender equality and the elimination of gender discrimination;
2. The integration and full participation of women in development; and

3. An increased contribution by women in the strengthening of world peace.

The conference adopted a World Plan of Action which offered guidelines for the governments and the international communities to follow for the next ten years in pursuit of the above three key objectives. India has endorsed the Mexico Plan of Action - 1975.

The Second World Conference on Women (Copenhagen Programme of Action –1980)

The second world conference was held in Copenhagen in 1980 to review and appraise or evaluate the 1975 World Plan of Action adopted in Mexico. A mention may be made here that the United Nations General Assembly adopted in 1979 the Convention on the Elimination of All Forms of Discrimination against Women, which was one of the most powerful instruments for women's equality. India ratified the Convention in 1993, as stated.

The Copenhagen Programme of Action called for, inter alia, stronger national measures to ensure women's ownership and control of property, women's right to inheritance, child custody and loss of nationality. The delegates at the Conference urged an end of the stereotyped attitudes towards women. In that Conference, legal rights and women's ability to exercise those rights were discussed. The Conference came to a close with the adoption of Programme of Action.

The Third World Conference on Women (Nairobi Forward - Looking Strategies – 1985)

The third world conference on women was

convened in Nairobi in 1985. The Conference has been referred to as the "birth of global feminism". The Conference was mainly to review and evaluate the achievements of the works of the United Nations on behalf of women. In that Conference, "Nairobi Forward-Looking Strategies" was adopted. In the Conference, it was declared that "all issues were to be women's issues". Keeping in view that all the issues were women's issues, measures recommended by the Strategies covered employment, health, education, social services, industry, science, communication and environment. The conference urged the governments to delegate responsibilities for women's issues to all the institutional offices.

The Fourth World Conference on Women (Beijing Declaration and Platform for Action – 1995)

The fourth world conference on women was convened in Beijing in September 1995, the year of the fiftieth anniversary of founding of the United Nations. In that Conference, the "Beijing Declaration and Platform for Action" was adopted. The Beijing Declaration indicates that the effort of the earlier three Conferences, namely Mexico Conference, Copenhagen Conference and Nairobi Conference, had helped to improve women's conditions and access to resources, but they had not able to change the basic structure of inequality in the relationship between men and women.

The Beijing Declaration recognized, reaffirmed and acknowledged, inter alia, that –

1. the status woman had advanced in some important respects in the past decade but that progress has been uneven, inequality between men and women have persisted and major obstacles remain;
2. the situation is exacerbated by the increasing poverty which is affecting lives of the majority of world's people, in particular women and children;
3. constraints and obstacles are enhancing further the advancement and empowerment of women all over the world;
4. women's empowerment and their full participation on the basis of equality in all spheres of society, including participation in the decision-making process and access to power, are fundamental for achievement of equality, development and peace;
5. women's rights are human rights; and
6. equal rights, opportunities and access to resources, equal sharing of responsibility of the family by men and women are important.

Thereafter, the governments participating the Fourth World Conference determined, inter alia, to—

1. intensify actions to achieve the full and effective implementation of the Nairobi Forward-Looking Strategies for the advancement of women;

2. ensure the full enjoyment by women and the girl-child of all human rights and fundamental freedoms and take effective action against the violations of these rights and freedoms;
3. take all necessary measure to eliminate all forms of discrimination against women and the girl child and remove all obstacles to gender inequality and advancement and empowerment of women;
4. encourage men to participate fully in all actions towards equality;
5. promote women's economic independence, including employment, and eradicate the persistent and increasing burden of poverty on women;
6. prevent and eliminate all forms violence against women and girls;
7. ensure equal access to and equal treatment of women and men in education and health care;
8. ensure women's equal access to economic resources, including land, credit, science and technology, vocational training, communication and markets, to further the advancement and empowerment of women and girls;
9. ensure to the women the empowerment and advancement of women, including the right to freedom of thoughts, conscience, religion and belief;

10. ensure the full implementation of human rights of women and of the girl-child and equal rights and inherent human dignity of women and men; and
11. ensure the success of the Platform for Action.

Critical Areas Representing Obstacle to Women's Advancement

Now, coming to the Beijing Platform for Action, the Beijing Platform for Action specified 12 critical areas in the sphere of human activities which represent the main obstacles to women's advancement and which required concrete action by the governments and civil societies. Those 12 critical areas are–

1. Women and Poverty;
2. Education and Training of Women;
3. Women and Health;
4. Violence against Women;
5. Women and Armed Conflict;
6. Women and the Economy;
7. Women in Power and Decision-making;
8. Institutional Mechanism for the Advancement of Women;
9. Human Rights of Women;
10. Women and the Media;
11. Women and the Environment;

12. The Girl-child.

The reasons for specifying 12 critical areas as obstacles to the advancement and empowerment of women and recommendations made to the governments (States Parties) to take action for removal of the obstacles are dealt with in the next chapter.

6

OBSTACLES TO ADVANCEMENT OF WOMEN AND FURTHER ACTIONS AND INITIATIVES TO IMPLEMENT THE BEIJING DECLARATION AND THE PLATFORM FOR ACTION

Preliminary

As stated, the Beijing Platform for Action has specified 12 critical areas in all spheres of human activities which represent the obstacles to the advancement and empowerment of women. The reasons for specifying the 12 areas as the obstacles and the recommendations made by the Beijing Platform Action for removal of the obstacles are stated in a few words hereafter;

1. Poverty

Today, more than one thousand million people live in extreme poverty and majority of them are women. The risk for falling into poverty is higher for women than for men, in particular women living in rural areas. Women are poorer because women have fewer economic opportunities and less autonomy than men.

Their access to economic resources education and training is limited. There are many factors, which have contributed to widening economic inequality between men and women. All harmful traditional and customary practices have also exacerbated or aggravated women's economic empowerment.

As stated, women are in the state of poverty, and that poverty makes an obstacle to the advancement and empowerment of women. Therefore, the Beijing Platform for Action has recommended the governments (States Parties) to take action, inter alia, to adopt and maintain macroeconomic policies and development strategies that address the needs and efforts of women in poverty; to ensure the women's right and access to economic resources; and to provide women with access to savings and credit mechanisms and institutions.

2. Education and Training

Education is a human right. Education is an indispensable element for economic and social progress, and it is also an essential tool or instrument for development of skills, abilities, mental power, moral standard etc. But girls in many countries still face discrimination due to customary or traditional attitudes, early marriages and pregnancies. Girls continue to be denied equality in education, in particular at higher education, say science and technology. However, formal and non-formal education and training for girls and women have been improved.

The lack of education and training of women, which is required for the promotion of women's status, also causes an obstruction to the advancement and empowerment of women. The Beijing Platform for Action has, therefore, recommended the governments (States Parties) to take action, inter alia, to ensure equal access to education; to eradicate illiteracy among women; and to improve women's access to vocational training, science and technology.

3. Health

Everywhere in the world, every minute of every day, a woman dies because of complications during pregnancy and childbirth. The majority of these deaths are preventable. According to World Health Organization (WHO), the annual global estimated toll is nearly 6,00,000 deaths and eight million cases of disability from pregnancy-related causes. In some countries, infections and communicable diseases continue to take a toll on women and girls. Investment in essential obstetric care remains insufficient in many countries. Women in many countries have unequal access to basic health resources. Girls receive less attention than boys in the prevention and treatment of childhood diseases. Women's rights to the highest standard of physical and mental health was recognized by the Fourth World Conference on Women in Beijing in 1995.

Poor health of women is one of the causes which prevents women's progress or development. The Beijing Platform for Action has, therefore, recommended the governments (States Parties) too take action, inter alia, to increase women's access throughout the life cycle to appropriate, affordable and quality health care, information and related services; to reduce maternal mortality; to encourage both women and men to take responsibility for their sexual and reproductive behaviour; to undertake gender-sensitive initiatives that address sexually transmitted diseases, HIV/AIDS etc. and to increase resources and monitor follow-up actions for women's health.

4. Violence

Women continue to be victims of various forms of violences, for example— domestic violence, rape, trafficking in women and girls, forced prostitution, honour killings, dowry-related violence, female infanticide and foeticide because of pre-natal sex selection in preference for male babies, female genital mutilation, sexual harassment at workplace and other places, and harmful practices and traditions. Violence against women and girls is a violation human rights and a form of discrimination against women.

Violence against women is another hindrance to the advancement of women and, therefore, the Beijing Platform for Action has recommended the governments (States Parties) to take action, inter alia, to adopt and implement legislation to end the violence against women; to ratify and implement all international agreements respecting violence against women, including the Convention on the Elimination of All Forms of Discrimination against Women, to adopt new laws and enforce existing ones to punish members of the security forces and police or any other state agents for acts of violence against women; to set up shelters, provide legal aid and other services for girls and women at risk, and provide counseling and rehabilitation for perpetrators of violence against women; and to step up national and international cooperation to dismantle networks engaged in trafficking in women.

5. Armed Conflict

Armed conflicts, war of aggression and terrorism are persisting in many parts of the world. Although entire communities suffer the consequences of armed conflict, women and girls are especially affected because of their sex. Rape is common during armed conflict. Other forms of violence against women in armed conflicts are murder, sexual slavery, forced pregnancy and forced sterilization.

The above consequences of armed conflict fall within one of the 12 critical areas specified in the Beijing Platform for Action, which represents the one of the obstacles to the advancement and empowerment of women. Therefore, the Platform for Action has recommended the governments (States Parties) to take action, inter alia, to increase the participation of women in conflict resolution at decision-making levels; to recognize the important roles and contributions of women in peace movement throughout the world; and to recognize the need to protect women living in situations of armed and other conflict.

6. Economy

Women are largely excluded from economic decision-making. Although there is increased participation of women in the labour market, women face low wages in the labour-market, poor working conditions and limited employment and professional opportunities. Their unpaid work, such as domestic and community work, is not measured in quantitative terms and not valued in national account.

The poor economic condition of women also makes impediment to the advancement of Women and, therefore, the Beijing Platform for Action has recommended the governments (States Parties) to take action, inter alia, to promote women's economic rights and independence, including access to employment and appropriate working conditions and control over economic resource; to facilitate women's equal access to resources, employments, markets and trades; and to promote harmonization of work and family responsibilities for man and women.

7. Decision-making

Despite the widespread movement for advancement and empowerment of women, women remain largely unrepresented at most level of government and other executive bodies and the target of having 30% of decision-making positions held by women by 1995, as endorsed by the UN Economic and Social Council, has not been reached showing slow progress. Apart from it, the unrepresentation of women in decision-making positions in the arts, culture, sports, the media, education, religion and law have prevented women from having a significant impact on many key institutions and policies. Traditionally assigned gender roles limit women's choices in education and careers and compel women to assume the burden for household responsibilities. Initiatives and programmes aimed at women's increased participation in decision-making were hindered by gender-sensitive attitudes towards women in society.

In the above view of the matters, the Beijing Platform for Action has recommended the governments (States Parties) to take actions, inter alia, to increase women's capacity to participate in decision-making and leadership positions; and to ensure women's equal access to and full participation in power structures and decision-making in governmental bodies and public administration entities, including the judiciary, international and non-governmental organizations, political parties and trade unions.

8. Institutional Mechanism

Most of the countries have established institutions for the advancement of women. But inadequate financial and human resources and a lack of political will and commitment are the main obstacles confronting national machineries. This is further exacerbated by insufficient understanding of gender equality, prevailing gender stereotypes rolls, discriminatory attitudes etc.

Considering the above, the Beijing Platform for Action has recommended the governments (States

Parties) to take action, inter alia, to create or strengthen national machineries and other governmental bodies; and to ensure that responsibility for the advancement of women is vested in the highest level of the government.

9. Human Rights

The full and equal enjoyment by women and girls is a priority of the governments and the United Nations, but women and girls have not been enjoying the full enjoyment of human rights and fundamental freedoms. Rape, domestic violence and other forms of violence mentioned above are violation of human rights and fundamental freedoms of the women and girls. There has been a lack of respect of human rights of women. Women are denied equality with men.

Under the above circumstance, the Beijing Platform for Action has recommended the government (States Parties) to take action, inter alia, to promote and protect human rights of women by fully implementing all human rights instruments, especially the Convention on the Elimination of All Forms of Discrimination against Women; to achieve legal literacy; and to review national laws to ensure implementation of all international human rights agreements.

10. Media

Today, many women work in the media, but few have reached positions at decision-making levels. In most of the countries, the media continue to project degrading image of women and do not reflect women's contribution to the society. The degrading images of women, including pornography, and stereotyped portrayals in different forms using new communication technologies in some cases show bias against women remains in the media. Women are also taking as journalists, reporters and broadcasters and, therefore, the Beijing Conference called for the empowerment of women through the enhancement of their skills, knowledge and access to information technologies.

The importance of the media has been indicated above and, therefore, the Beijing Platform for Action has recommended the governments (States Parties) to take actions, inter alia, to increase women's participation in and access to expression and decision-making in and through the media and new technologies of communication; and to promote a balanced and non-stereotyped portrayal of women in the media.

11. Environment

Women's participation in the formulation, planning and execution of environmental policy continues to be low. At the same time, the international community feels that without women's full participation, sustainable development cannot be achieved, because women have a key role to play in preserving the environment and natural resources, and in promoting sustainable development. For example, women still have the main responsibility for meeting household needs and are therefore a major force in determining consumption trends, that is to say – through their management and use of natural resources, women provide sustenance to their family and communities. Beijing Conference identified the need to actively involve women in the environmental decision-making at all levels as one of the 12 critical areas of concern requiring actions by the government, the international community and civil society.

For the reasons stated above, the Beijing Platform for Action has recommended the governments (States Parties) to take action, inter alia, to involve women actively in environmental decision-making at all levels; and to strengthen or establish mechanisms at the national, regional and international levels to assess the impact of development and environment policies on women.

12. Girl-child

In many countries, the girl-child faces discrimination from earliest stage of life. Her low status is reflected in the denial of fundamental needs and rights such as less food and less access to education. Overall, girls' school attendance still lags severely behind those of boys. One of the major reasons why so many girls do not attend school is because of their workload, both within and outside the household. When a girl is prevented from going to school or is too exhausted to pay attention in class because of her houseload at home, she is being denied her right to education. Girls are often kept at home to help family because the social and economic values of educating girls is not recognized. Girls are treated as inferior to boys, both within the home and by society -at-large. They are socialized to put themselves last. Girls and their mothers are often last to be fed, resulting in a diet low in calories and protein. However, the educated mothers usually have smaller family, with healthier and better-educated children.

Violence against girls and women remains a persistent problem that takes many forms, including sexual exploitation and abuse, rape, incest, prostitution, child pornography, trafficking, and harmful traditional practice such as female genital mutilation. Girls are also more vulnerable than boys to the consequences of unprotected and premature sexual relations, including HIV/AIDS. There has been an alarming increase in number of girls infected with HIV virus.

Because of the discrimination which girl-child faces, the Beijing Platform for Action has recommended the governments (States Parties) to take actions, inter alia, to eliminate all forms of discrimination against girl-child; to enact and enforce appropriate legislation that guarantees equal rights to succession, regardless of sex of the child; to eliminate discrimination against girls in education, skills, and development and training, including health and nutrition; to eliminate the economic exploitation of a child labour and protect young girls at work; and to strengthen the role of the family in improving the status of the girl-child.

Further Actions and Initiatives to Implement the Beijing Declaration and the Platform for Action

In the 23rd special session of the United Nations

General Assembly in 2000, while adopting "Further actions and initiatives to implement the Beijing Declaration and the Platform for Action", the governments which came together reaffirmed their commitment to the goals and objectives contained in the Beijing Declaration and the Platform for Action, which was adopted in 1995.

The governments reviewed and appraised progress and identified obstacles and current challenges in the implementation of Platform for Action. They recognized that the goals and commitments made in the Platform of Action have not been fully implemented and achieved and have agreed upon further actions and initiatives at local, national, regional, and international levels to accelerate its implementations. The Platform for Action, together with the agreed conclusions and recommendations, forms the basis for further progress towards the achievement of gender equality, development and peace. The Platform for Action emphasizes that women share common concerns that can be addressed only by working together and in partnership with men towards common goals of gender equality around the world; and many women encountered obstacles related to their family traditions. The assessment shows that even though significant positive development can be identified, obstacles or barriers remain and, therefore, there is still need to further implement the goals and commitments made in Beijing. What are the actions to be taken by the governments (States Parties) at national level and what are those to be taken at the international level are described in the "Further actions and initiatives to implement the Beijing Declaration and the Platform for Action".

7

NATIONAL POLICY FOR EMPOWERMENT OF WOMEN, 2001

Introduction

After the Beijing Declaration and the Platform for Action, the "Further actions and initiatives to implement the Beijing Declaration and the Platform for Action" was adopted by the United Nations General Assembly in the 23rd special session in 2002, as stated.

As stated, India endorsed the "Further actions and initiatives to implement the Beijing Declarations and the Platform for Action" and, therefore, India has become one of the States Parties to the Conference. It has also been stated that the Beijing Declaration and the Platform for Action could not be fully implemented and achieved, and that the further actions and initiatives are to be taken at the national and international levels. What are the actions which are to be taken by the governments (States Parties) and what are those which are to be taken at international levels have been formulated in the "Further actions and initiatives to implement the Beijing Declarations and the Platform for Action".

National Policy— 2001

In view of the above, the "National Policy for the Empowerment of Women, 2001" (hereinafter the "National Policy") was brought out by the Government of India, as a follow-up to the "Further actions and initiatives to implement the Beijing Declarations and the Platform for Action". The "National Policy" was to be widely disseminated so as to encourage active participation of all the stakeholders for achieving its goals.

Goals and Objectives

The National Policy begins with the preliminary under the heading **"Introduction",** and it has been followed by the "aims and objects" of the National Policy under the heading **"Goals and Objectives".** The National Policy has described under 16 major heads the measures to be taken by the Government of India. Those 16 major heads are –

(1) Policy Prescriptions;

(2) Decision Making;

(3) Mainstreaming a Gender Perspective in the Development Process;

(4) Economic Empowerment of Women;

(5) Social Empowerment of Women;

(6) Violence against Women;

(7) Rights of the Girl Child;

(8) Mass Media;

(9) Operational Strategies;

(10) Institutional Mechanisms;

(11) Resource Management;

(12) Legislation;

(13) Gender Sensitisation;

(14) Panchayati Raj Institutions;

(15) Partnership with the voluntary sector organization; and

(16) International Cooperation.

The full text of the National Policy for Women is set out at Appendix- III; and the details of the National Policy are indicated in Appendix- III. However, the gist of the National Policy under the above-mentioned headings are as follows.

1. Introduction

Plans and programmes have aimed at women's advancement in different spheres. In recent years, the empowerment of women has been recognised as a central issue in determining the status of women. The National Commission for Women Act 1990 was enacted by the Parliament to safeguard the rights and legal entitlements of women. The Constitution Amendments made in 1993 have provided for reservation of seats in the local bodies of Panchayats and Municipalities for women, laying a strong foundation for their participation in decision-making at the local levels.

India has also ratified various international conventions and human rights instruments committing to secure equal rights of women. Key among them is the ratification of the Convention on the Elimination of All Forms of Discrimination against Women (CEDAW) in 1993. The Mexico Plan of Action (1975), the Nairobi Forward-Looking Strategies (1985), the Beijing Declaration as well as the Platform for Action (1995) and the "Further actions and initiatives to implement the Beijing Declaration and the Platform for Action" have been unreservedly endorsed by India for appropriate follow-up.

However, there still exists a wide gap between the goals enunciated in the Constitution, legislation, policies, plans, programmes, and related mechanisms on the one hand and the situational reality of the status of women in India, on the other. Gender disparity manifests itself in various forms, the most obvious being the trend of continuously declining female ratio in the population in the last few decades.

The underlying causes of gender inequality are related to social and economic structure. The access of women particularly those belonging to weaker sections including Scheduled Castes/Scheduled Tribes/ Other Backward Classes and minorities, majority of whom are in the rural areas and in the informal or unorganised sector,— to education, health and productive resources. Therefore, they remain largely marginalised, poor and socially excluded.

2. Goals and Objectives

The goal of the National Policy is to bring about

the advancement, development and empowerment of women. The Policy will be widely disseminated so as to encourage active participation of all stakeholders for achieving its goals. Specifically, the objectives of this Policy include — (i) Creating an environment through positive economic and social policies for full development of women to enable them to realise their full potential; (ii) The enjoyment of all human rights and fundamental freedom by women on equal basis with men in all spheres— political, economic, social, cultural and civil; (iii) Equal access to participation and decision-making of women in social, political and economic life of the nation; (iv) Equal access to women to health care, quality education at all levels, career and vocational guidance, employment, equal remuneration, occupational health and safety, social security and public office etc; (v) Strengthening legal systems aimed at elimination of all forms of discrimination against women; (vi) Changing societal attitudes and community practices by active participation and involvement of both men and women; (vii) Mainstreaming a gender perspective in the development process; (viii) Elimination of discrimination and all forms of violence against women and the girl child; and (ix) Building and strengthening partnerships with civil society, particularly women's organisations.

3. Policy Prescriptions
Judicial Legal Systems

Legal-judicial system will be made more responsive and gender- sensitive to women's needs, especially in cases of domestic violence and personal assault. New laws will be enacted and existing laws reviewed to ensure that justice is quick. The Policy would aim at encouraging changes in personal laws such as those related to marriage, divorce, maintenance and guardianship so as to eliminate discrimination against women, as well as encouraging change in laws relating to ownership of property and inheritance by evolving consensus in order to make them gender just.

4. Decision-making

Women's equality in power sharing and active participation in decision-making, including decision-making in political process at all levels will be ensured for the achievement of the goals of empowerment. All measures will be taken to guarantee women equal access to and full participation in decision-making bodies at every level, including the legislative, executive, judicial, corporate, statutory bodies, as also the advisory Commissions, Committees, Boards, Trusts etc.

5. Mainstreaming a Gender Perspective in the Development Process

Policies, programmes and systems will be established to ensure mainstreaming of women's perspectives in all developmental processes, as catalysts, participants and recipients. Wherever there are gaps in policies and programmes, women specific interventions would be undertaken to bridge these. Women's issues and concerns as a result will specially be addressed and reflected in all concerned laws, sectoral policies, plans and programmes of action.

6. Economic Empowerment of Women

6.1. *Poverty Eradication*

Women comprise the majority of the population below the poverty line and are very often in situations of extreme poverty. Therefore, macroeconomic policies and poverty eradication programmes will specifically address the needs and problems of such women. Steps will be taken for mobilisation of poor women and convergence of services, by offering them a range of economic and social options, along with necessary support measures to enhance their capabilities.

6.2. *Micro-Credit*

In order to enhance women's access to credit for consumption and production, the establishment of new, and strengthening of existing micro-credit mechanisms and micro-finance institutions will be undertaken so that the outreach of credit is enhanced.

6.3. *Women and Economy*

Women's perspectives will be included in designing and implementing macroeconomic and social policies by institutionalising their participation in such processes. Their contribution to socio-economic development as producers and workers will be recognised in the formal and informal sectors (including home based workers) and appropriate policies relating to employment and to her working conditions will be drawn up.

6.4. *Globalisation*

Globalisation has presented new challenges for the

realisation of the goal of women's equality, the gender impact of which has not been systematically evaluated fully. Strategies will be designed to enhance the capacity of women and empower them to meet the negative social and economic impacts, which may flow from the globalisation process.

6.5. *Women and Agriculture*

In view of the critical role of women in the agriculture and allied sectors, as producers, concentrated efforts will be made to ensure that benefits of training, extension and various programmes will reach them in proportion to their numbers. The programmes for training women in soil conservation, social forestry, dairy development and other occupations allied to agriculture like horticulture, livestock including small animal husbandry, poultry, fisheries etc, will be expanded to benefit women workers in the agriculture sector.

6.6. *Women and Industry*

The important role played by women in electronics, information technology, food processing, agro industry and textiles has been crucial to the development of these sectors. They would be given comprehensive support in terms of labour legislation, social security and other support services to participate in various industrial sectors.

Women at present cannot work in night shift in factories even if they wish to. Suitable measures will be taken to enable women to work in night shift in factories. This will be accompanied with support services for security, transportation etc.

6.7. *Support Services*

The provision of support services for women, like child care facilities, creches at work places and educational institutions, homes for the aged and the disabled will be expanded and improved to create an enabling environment and to ensure their full cooperation in social, political and economic life.

7. Social Empowerment of Women

7.1. *Education*

Equal access to education for women and girls will be ensured. Special measures will be taken to eliminate discrimination, universalise education, eradicate illiteracy, create a gender-sensitive educational system, increase enrolment and retention rates of girls and improve the quality of education to facilitate life-long learning as well as development of vocational/technical skills by women. Gender-sensitive curricula would be developed at all levels of educational system in order to address sex stereotyping as one of the causes of gender discrimination.

7.2. *Health*

A holistic approach to women's health which includes both nutrition and health services will be adopted and special attention will be given to the needs of women and the girl at all stages of the life cycle. The reduction of infant mortality and maternal mortality, which are sensitive indicators of human development, is a priority concern. Women should have access to comprehensive, affordable and quality health care. The social, developmental and health consequences of HIV/AIDS and other sexually transmitted diseases will be tackled from a gender perspective.

To effectively meet problems of infant and maternal mortality, and early marriage, the availability of good and accurate data at micro-level on deaths, birth and marriages is required. Strict implementation of registration of births and deaths would be ensured and registration of marriages would be made compulsory. The Policy recognises the critical need of men and women to have access to safe, effective and affordable methods of family planning of their choice and the need to suitably address the issues of early marriages and spacing of children.

Women's traditional knowledge about health care and nutrition will be recognised through proper documentation and its use will be encouraged. The use of Indian and alternative systems of medicine will be enhanced within the framework of overall health infrastructure available for women.

7.3. *Nutrition*

In view of the high risk of malnutrition and disease that women face at all the three critical stages, viz infancy and childhood, adolescent and reproductive phase, focussed attention would be paid to meeting the nutritional needs of women at all stages of the life cycle. This is also important in view of the critical link between the health of adolescent girls, pregnant and lactating women with the health of infant and young children. Special efforts will be made to tackle the problem of nutrient deficiencies, especially amongst pregnant and lactating women as it leads to various diseases and disabilities.

Intra-household discrimination in nutritional matters vis-a-vis girls and women will be sought to be ended through appropriate strategies. Widespread use of nutrition education would be made to address the issues of intra-household imbalances in nutrition and the special needs of pregnant and lactating women. Women's participation will also be ensured in the planning, superintendence and delivery of the system.

7.4. *Drinking Water and Sanitation*

Special attention will be given to the needs of women in the provision of safe drinking water, sewage disposal, toilet facilities and sanitation within accessible reach of households, especially in rural areas and urban slums. Women's participation will be ensured in the planning, delivery and maintenance of such services.

7.5. *Housing and Shelter*

Women's perspectives will be included in the housing policies, planning of housing colonies and provision of shelter both in rural and urban areas. Special attention will be given for providing adequate and safe housing and accommodation for women including single women, heads of households, working women, students, apprentices and trainees.

7.6. *Environment*

Women will be involved and their perspectives

reflected in the polices and programmes for environment, conservation and restoration. Considering the impact of environmental factors on their livelihoods, women's participation will be ensured in the conservation of the environment and control of environmental degradation. The vast majority of rural women still depend on the locally available non-commercial sources of energy such as animal dung, crop waste and fuel wood. In order to ensure the efficient use of these energy resources in an environmental friendly manner, the Policy will aim at promoting the programmes of non-conventional energy resources. Women will be involved in spreading the use of solar energy, biogas, smokeless chulahs and other rural application so as to have a visible impact of these measures in influencing ecosystem and in changing the life styles of rural women.

7.7. *Science and Technology*

Programmes will be strengthened to bring about a greater involvement of women in science and technology. These will include measures to motivate girls to take up science and technology for higher education and also ensure that development projects with scientific and technical inputs involve women fully. Efforts to develop a scientific temper and awareness will also be stepped up. Special measures would be taken for their training in areas where they have special skills like communication and information technology. Efforts to develop appropriate technologies suited to women's needs as well as to reduce their drudgery will be given a special focus too.

7.8. *Women in Difficult Circumstances*

In recognition of the diversity of women's situations and in acknowledgment of the needs of specially disadvantaged groups, measures and programmes will be undertaken to provide them with special assistance. These groups include women in extreme poverty, destitute women, women in conflict situations, women affected by natural calamities, women in less developed regions, the disabled widows, elderly women, single women in difficult circumstances, women heading households, those displaced from employment, migrants, women who are victims of marital violence, deserted women and prostitutes etc.

8. Violence against Women

All forms of violence against women, physical and mental, whether at domestic or societal levels, including those arising from customs, traditions or accepted practices shall be dealt with effectively with a view to eliminate its incidence. Institutions and mechanisms/schemes for assistance will be created and strengthened for prevention of such violence, including sexual harassment at work place and customs like dowry; for the rehabilitation of the victims of violence and for taking effective action against the perpetrators of such violence. A special emphasis will also be laid on programmes and measures to deal with trafficking in women and girls.

9. Rights of the Girl Child

All forms of discrimination against the girl child

and violation of her rights shall be eliminated by undertaking strong measures both preventive and punitive within and outside the family. These would relate specifically to strict enforcement of laws against pre-natal sex selection and the practices of female foeticide, female infanticide, child marriage, child abuse and child prostitution etc. Removal of discrimination in the treatment of the girl child within the family and outside, and projection of a positive image of the girl child will be actively fostered. There will be special emphasis on the needs of the girl child and earmarking of substantial investments in the areas relating to food and nutrition, health and education, and in vocational education. In implementing programmes for eliminating child labour, there will be a special focus on girl children.

10. Mass Media

Media will be used to portray images consistent with human dignity of girls and women. The Policy will specifically strive to remove demeaning, degrading and negative conventional stereotypical images of women and violence against women. The media would be encouraged to develop codes of conduct, professional guidelines and other self regulatory mechanisms to remove gender stereotypes and promote balanced portrayals of women and men.

11. Operational Strategies
Action Plans

All Central and State Ministries will draw up time bound Action Plans for translating the Policy into a set of concrete actions, through a participatory process of consultation with Centre/State Departments of Women and Child Development and National/State Commissions for Women.

In order to support better planning and programme formulation and adequate allocation of resources, Gender Development Indices (GDI) will be developed by networking with specialised agencies. These could be analysed and studied in depth. Gender auditing and development of evaluation mechanisms will also be undertaken along side.

Collection of gender disaggregated data by all primary data collecting agencies of the Central and State Governments as well as Research and Academic Institutions in the public and private sectors will be undertaken.

12. Institutional Mechanisms

Institutional mechanisms, to promote the advancement of women, which exist at the Central and State levels, will be strengthened. National and State Councils will be formed to oversee the operationalisation of the Policy on a regular basis. The National Council will be headed by the Prime Minister and the State Councils by the Chief Ministers and will be broad in composition having representatives from the concerned Departments/Ministries, National and State Commissions for Women, Social Welfare Boards, representatives of Non-Government Organisations, Women's Organisations, Corporate Sector, Trade Unions, financing institutions, academics experts and social activists etc. These bodies will review the progress made in implementing the Policy twice a year. The National Development Council will also be informed of the progress of the programme undertaken under the policy from time to time for advice and comments.

National and State Resource Centres on women will be established with mandates for collection and dissemination of information, undertaking research work, conducting surveys, implementing training and awareness generation programmes etc. While institutions at the district level will be strengthened, at the grassroots, women will be helped by Government through its programmes to organise and strengthen into Self-Help Groups (SHGs) at the Anganwadi Village/Town level. The women's groups will be helped to institutionalise themselves into registered societies and to federate at the Panchayat/ Municipal level. These societies will bring about synergistic implementation of all the social and economic development programmes by drawing resources made available through Government and Non-governmental channels, including banks and financial institutions and by establishing a close interface with the Panchayats/Municipalities.

13. Resource Management

Availability of adequate financial, human and market resources to implement the Policy will be managed by concerned Departments, financial credit institutions and banks, private sector, civil society and other connected institutions. The Department of

Women and Child Development being the nodal Ministry will monitor and review the progress of the implementation of the Component Plan from time to time, in terms of both quality and quantity, in collaboration with the Planning Commission.

14. Legislation

The existing legislative structure will be reviewed and additional legislative measures taken by identified departments to implement the Policy. This will also involve a review of all existing laws including personal, customary and tribal laws, subordinate legislation, related rules as well as executive and administrative regulations to eliminate all gender discriminatory references.

Effective implementation of legislation would be promoted by involving civil society and community. Appropriate changes in legislation will be undertaken, if necessary. In addition, the following specific measures will be taken to implement the legislation effectively:

(a) Strict enforcement of all relevant legal provisions and speedy redressal of grievances will be ensured, with a special focus on violence and gender related atrocities;

(b) Measures to prevent and punish sexual harassment at the place of work, protection for women workers in the organised/unorganised sector and strict enforcement of relevant laws such as Equal Remuneration Act and Minimum Wages Act will be undertaken;

(c) Crimes against women, their incidence, prevention, investigation, detection and prosecution will be regularly reviewed at all Crime Review fora and Conferences at the Central, State and District levels. Recognised local, voluntary organisations will be authorised to lodge complaints and facilitate registration, investigations and legal proceedings related to violence and atrocities against girls and women;

(d) Women's Cells in Police Stations, Women Police Stations, Family Courts, Mahila Courts, Counselling Centres, Legal Aid Centres and Nyaya Panchayats will be strengthened and expanded to eliminate violence and atrocities against women;

(e) Widespread dissemination of information on all aspects of legal rights, human rights and other entitlements of women, through specially designed legal literacy programmes and rights information programmes will be done.

15. Gender Sensitisation

Training of personnel of executive, legislative and judicial wings of the State, with a special focus on policy and programme framers, implementation and development agencies, law enforcement machinery and the judiciary, as well as non-governmental organisations will be undertaken.

16. Panchayati Raj Institutions

The 73rd and 74th Amendments (1993) to the

Indian Constitution have served as a breakthrough towards ensuring equal access and increased participation in political power structure for women. The Panchayati Raj Institutions will play a central role in the process of enhancing women's participation in public life. The Panchayati Raj Institutions and the local self governments will be actively involved in the implementation and execution of the National Policy for Women at the grassroots level.

17. Partnership with the Voluntary Sector Organisations

The involvement of voluntary organisations, associations, federations, trade unions, non-governmental organisations, women's organisations, as well as institutions dealing with education, training and research will be ensured in the formulation, implementation, monitoring and review of all policies and programmes affecting women. Towards this end, they will be provided with appropriate support related to resources and capacity building and facilitated to participate actively in the process of the empowerment of women.

18. International Cooperation

The Policy will aim at implementation of international obligations/commitments in all sectors on empowerment of women such as the Convention on the Elimination of All Forms of Discrimination against Women (CEDAW), Convention on the Rights of the Child (CRC), International Conference on Population and Development (ICPD) and other such instruments. International, regional and sub-regional cooperation towards the empowerment of women will continue to be encouraged through sharing of experiences, exchange of ideas and technology, networking with institutions and organisations and through bilateral and multilateral partnerships.

8

OBSERVATION ON THE NATIONAL POLICY

Introduction

As stated, the National Policy is, or in the nature of, a follow-up to the "Further actions and initiatives to implement the Beijing Declaration and the Platform for Action" in view of the provision thereunder providing actions to be taken by the governments (State Parties). The National Policy includes some of the 12 critical areas specified in the Beijing Platform for Action.

Women's Ability to Exercise Their Rights

The Para 1.11(ii) of the National Policy shows that the "enjoyment of all human rights and fundamental freedom by women on equal basis with men in all spheres – political, economic, social and cultural and civil", whereas the CEDAW has given emphasis on "political, economics, social, cultural, civil or **any other fields** for the enjoyment of human rights and fundamental freedom, while defining "discrimination against women". The expression **"any other fields"** is a very wide term. As stated, women and men cannot be equal in all the spheres of human activities and in all situations. For example —Para 5.7 of the National Policy reads: "Women at present cannot work in night shift in factories even if they wish to". Therefore, the question which arises is about the ability of women to exercise their legal rights. However, in the field where men and women are to be treated as equal, the term **"any other fields"** shall be attracted because the expression "all forms of discrimination" has been used in both the CEDAW and the National Policy.

Fundamental Freedoms etc

In the National Policy, the enjoyment of human rights and fundamental freedom by the women on equal basis with men has been limited to political, economic, social, cultural and civil rights or spheres. In the context of the National Policy –

(1) "Political right" is a right exercisable in the establishment or administration of government, without distinction between men and women.

(2) "Economic right" is a right that there shall not be no distinction between men and women from the stand point of economic value, that is to say – equality of reward for equal work, every men should get his just dues for his labour, irrespective sex or social position, including the abolition of those economic conditions which results in the inequality of economic value between men and women.

(3) "Social right" points to the absence of

discrimination made between one group and another or one class of persons and another on the grounds of birth, wealth, sex etc, ie the abolition of all source of inequality, and it includes provisions for humane conditions of work such as maternity relief, paternity relief, offering leisure and cultural opportunities to every individual, prevention of exploitation of child in labour and industry, provisions for free primary education for all, the promotion of the educational and economic interest of backward class etc.

(4) "Cultural right" is a right of way of life, arts and customs that are shared and accepted by the people in a particular society, as distinct from legal rights and obligations. Culture thus consists of language, ideas, beliefs, customs, work of arts, rituals, ceremonies etc.

(5) "Civil right" is a right accorded to every member of a community or nation relating to property, family or marriage, and the like.

Primary Importance of the National Policy

The National Policy is for eradication of gender injustice in all spheres — political, economics, social, cultural and civil, and these are indispensable elements for human existence in the modern society. But, in the **"Introduction"** of the National Policy, it has been stated : "The underlying causes of gender inequality are related to **social and economic structure**", and the **"Goals and Objectives"** of the

National Policy shows that one of the objectives is "Creation an environment through **positive economic and social policy"**. Therefore, the National Policy has given primary importance or special attention to the **social and economic structure or policy** to protect gender inequality, in the context of India. The National Policy is one of the strongest instruments brought out by the Government of India for gender justice.

Enactment of Laws

As regards Enactment of laws for the achievement of the National Policy, many substantive and procedural laws have been amended, and new laws have been enacted. For example—-

1. The Hindu Succession Act has been amended by the Hindu Succession Amendment Act of 2005, which came into force on 09.09.2005, to make men and women have the same right to property making gender just.

2. Against men's oppression of women, the Parliament has enacted an Act respecting "Domestic Violence" called as the "Protection of Women from Domestic Violence Act of 2005", which came into force wef 26.10.2006. This Act applies not only to wife, but also all women sharing a household with a man such as live-partners, daughters, sisters, mothers and widows living together as a joint family, which comes within the meaning of **"domestic relationship"**, as defined in the Act. In the

Act, the word **"respondent"** means "any adult male person who is, or has been, in a domestic relationship with the aggrieved person and against whom the aggrieved person has sought any relief under this Act; Provided that aggrieved wife or female living in a relationship in the nature of a marriage may also file complaint against a relative of the husband or the male partner". The expression **"aggrieved person"** has been defined in the Act to mean "any women who is, or has been in a domestic relationship with the respondent and who alleges to have been subjected to any act of domestic violence by the respondent".

Domestic Violence;– Any act, omission or commission or conduct of the respondent shall constitute domestic violence in case it—

(a) harms or injures or endangers the health, safety, life, limb or well-being, whether mental and physical, of the aggrieved person or tends to do so and includes causing **physical abuse, sexual abuse, verbal and emotional abuse and economic abuse**; or

b) harasses, harms, injures or endangers the aggrieved person with a view to coerce her or any other person related to her to meet any unlawful demand for any dowry or other property or valuable security; or

(c) has the effect of threatening the aggrieved person or any person related to her by any conduct mentioned in clause (a) or clause (b); or

(d) otherwise injures or causes harm, whether physical or mental, to the aggrieved person.

Physical abuse, sexual abuse, verbal and emotional abuse and economic abuse has been explained in the Act. It appears that marital rape has been made as an offence for the first time in the history of penal law.

The aggrieved person, who has been subjected to any act of domestic violence, can complain to concerned Protection Officer (appointed under the Act), Service Provider (registered under the Act), Police Officer and Magistrate. The aggrieved person shall be entitled, inter alia, to the following reliefs –

1. free legal services under the Legal Services Authorities Act, 1987;
2. shelter homes and medical facilities;
3. right to reside in a shared household;
4. protection orders from the Magistrate;
5. monetary reliefs for loss of earning etc.;
6. compensation and damages for injuries etc;

It is one of the most powerful Act for removing or eradicating domestic violence which is very common in India. If this Act is fully implemented the basic domestic violence against women will more or less go away or disappear.

3 The Parliament has also enacted the "Micro, Small and Medium Enterprises Development Act, 2006". That act has defined "**enterprise**", including micro enterprise, small enterprise and medium enterprise. That Act has also provided for credit facilities and constitution of one or more funds for the purpose of credit facilities. It is internationally accepted that the provision of credit, especially micro-credit, has become a very popular and successful strategy for poverty eradication, as stated. It may be stated that the National Policy has assured that the micro-credit mechanisms will be strengthened in order to enhance women's access to credit for consumption and production, and that women's group will be helped to Institutionalised themselves into registered society. The CEDAW has also emphasised to organize **self-help groups and co-operatives** in order to obtain equal access to economic opportunities through employment or self employment. In other to prevent form misusing the funds by the beneficiaries, discussions in various forms about the utility of the funds or money in credits and the establishment of any enterprise are very essential to meet the realities in life. If the women utilise the money in credit, especially micro-credit, sincerely and honestly, the poverty of women shall be eradicated to a large extent.

In Addition

Furthermore, the following may further be viewed by the persons or the authorities concerned with the National Policy —

A. As stated, para 5.7 of the National Policy reads: "Women at present cannot work in night shift in factories even if they wish to ". This shows that equal opportunities in the matters relating to employment does not, however, mean that men and women are equal in all occupations and in all situation; and that men and women are not equal in all the fields of human existence, as stated. Therefore, where there is equal rights for men and women in the matters relating to employment and other fields, the question as to women's ability to exercise their right arises. It is because of their sex or sex consciousness or sex psychology. All the difficulties which women face in the enjoyment of human rights and fundamental freedoms respecting political, economic, social, cultural and civil aspects should be removed so that women can enjoy their rights to achieve the goals of the National Policy. In that para 5.7 of the National Policy, the Government of India has promised: "Suitable measures will be taken to enable women to work in night shift in factories. This will be accompanied with support services for security, transportation etc". What are the support services for women are indicated in para 5.8 of the National Policy. If the aforesaid measures are taken up for all the States in India, it will improve women's economy and other related status of women to a very large extent.

B. Paras 2.1, 13.2 and 13.3 of the National Policy relate to implementation legislation. On a reading of the three paragraphs, it shows that laws are not implemented to the satisfaction of the authorities or persons concerned. Today, there are sufficient laws in India for protection of gender inequality. The policy has undertaken that new laws whenever required and necessary will be made and existing law shall be reviewed because of changing social realities. Even if the existing laws are enforced effectively, there will be sufficient improvement of the gender justice. Therefore, it is not the absence of law, but the lack of implementation of laws, which results in failure to protect gender inequality. For example, foeticides because of pre-natal sex selection in favour of male babies, which is against one of the most stringent existing law, namely the Pre-Natal Diagnostic Techniques (Regulation and Prevention of Misuse) Act of 1994, which prohibits sex determination of a foetus (see sec 6 of the Act), are still in practice in India. The abortion or foeticide in preference for male babies and female infanticide, which are now prevailing in India, are the main cause of declining female ratio in the population, as indicated in para 1.8 of the National Policy. A mention may be made here that pre-natal diagnostic techniques is to be conducted for the purpose of detecting abnormalities described in the Act, and not for determining the sex of the foetus (see sec 4 of that Act). Then— How does such foeticides occur? Is it because of the manipulation between the doctors and husbands of the pregnant women? Is it because of the negligence of the authorities mentioned in the Act ? Answer is for the government. It is only one of the instances of the lack of implementation of laws. The National Policy assures that relevant women-related laws will be strictly implemented, including strict enforcement of laws against pre-natal sex selection and practices of female infanticide. To what extent it would be possible considering the present position in some parts of this country about the officials or persons who are open to corruption; it is a known fact. Corruption is the main cause of maladministration. If the maladministration is not eliminated the country shall be in peril or danger. The power-intoxicated authoritarian persons are the main cause of these happenings.

C. Today, more than 1000 million people live in extreme poverty and majority of them are women. Para 5.1 of the National Policy shows that women are below poverty line and are very often in situations of extreme poverty. As stated, out of a large segment of society which have been traditionally subjected to unjust treatment, women are one of such segment, and women are backward in education and political performance. The para 5 series of the National Policy have indicated measures to be taken by the Government for eradication of the poverty of women. At any event, the programmes are as per the desire of the international communities. As stated, it is now internationally accepted that the provision of credit, especially micro-credit, has become a very popular and successful strategy for poverty eradication. Therefore, the Micro, Small and Medium Enterprises Development Act 2006 will help in the eradication of women's poverty. It is to be seen to what extent programmes indicated in the National Policy are successfully implemented.

D. One of the causes of the gender inequality is the harmful traditions, usages or practices, as indicated in the CEDAW. Under the CEDAW, one of the measures (including legislation) to be taken by the States Parties is "to modify or abolish existing laws, regulations, customs and practices which constitute discrimination against women" [see Article 2(f)]. The National Policy also indicate similar idea [see paras 1.11(vi) and 2.2 of the National Policy]. Traditional attitudes still prevails in many cultures on the one hand, and the conservation of culture is one of the fundamental rights under Article 29 of the Constitution, on the other. But there are many harmful culture and traditions or customs prescribing what women should do and what should not do, as stated.

The traditional attitudes or views still prevails in many cultures in the world. In other words, an individual's attitudes, ideals, beliefs etc. are greatly influenced by the culture or cultures in which she or he lives. The question then is: Whether we the people living in the modern and advanced society should go back to the ways of life in the primitive society and follow the primitive views or primitive feelings. History tells us that primitive feelings are not based on reasons, and seem to come from a part of people's character that is ancient and animal-like.

It is seen that culture changes have been taking place in many countries because of socioeconomic, political, ecological and religious factors affecting a society. Therefore, people living in the modern world, including India, have encountered their harmful family or community traditions. As stated, there are many women today who are successful doctors, engineers, teachers, planners, managers, politicians, pilots etc, who had encountered their harmful family or community traditions. Situated thus, those traditions which make obstructions to the idea of equal enjoyment of political, social, economic, cultural and civil rights by women on equal basis with men should be made out-dated by legislation or otherwise. It is also one of the objectives of the National Policy [see Para I.11 (vi)].

Customs, traditions, practices or usages which are opposed to public policy or laws are invalid, it is settled. The public policy is equality of men and women in enjoyment of the political, economic, social, cultural and civil rights or spheres; and the laws are principles of gender equality as enshrined in the Indian Constitution, women-related laws, international Conventions, Covenants and Declarations mentioned somewhere above. A mention may be made here that the Courts in India view that International Instruments are to be respected by all signatories.

In view of the above, those traditions, customs, usages or practices which are opposed to public policy or laws are invalid. Because of cultural, ethnic, linguistic etc diversity in India, if no legislation can be made, the direct result can be achieved in some cases only when women themselves sponsor the cause in order to change the attitudes or views towards women. It may be through appropriate Courts as provided under the Constitution.

E. Para 2.2 of the National Policy indicates full participation of "community and religion leaders" for changes in personal laws such as marriage, divorce, maintenance and guardianship so as to eliminate discrimination against women. Normally, community leaders have extreme political idea and religion leaders have extreme religious idea; and they represent a real danger to democracy, it is said. They may be requested for the full participation as suggested in para 2.2 referred to above. They are heads of the modern and advanced society in their respective areas. They may agree to the request seeing the changing social realities. If they do not agree to the request– there are alternatives as suggested above.

F. In general, women are assuming household responsibility, especially in India. Women and girl-child are looking after the house and people therein. This affects the women and girl-child in various areas falling within the 12 critical areas described in the Beijing Platform Action, and it will be an obstacle to the objectives provided under the National Policy. As stated, women and girl-child still have the main responsibility for meeting household needs. Girl-child is unable to pay attention in the class because of her house load at home, and, therefore, drop-out rate is more than the boys. This matter cannot be done away within one or two days.

In para No.1.11 (vi) of the National Policy, it is stated: "Changing societal attitudes and community practices by active participation and involvement of both men and women". It is more or less in terms of International Instruments, and this is also one of the essentials for achieving the goal under the National Policy. The Beijing Declaration has emphasised on "equal sharing of responsibility of the family by men and women" and "to encourage men to participate fully in all actions towards equality", and the Platform for Action has also given stress on "by working together and in partnership with men". The National Policy has also made a provision for "gender sensitisation" (see para 14). These are principles only; and these principles are to be translated into realities in life. A systematic discussion on "of gender bias", especially in partnership with voluntary organizations, may solve the problem to a great extent. The above is in adition to what have been stated that the direct result can be achieved if women themselves sponsor the cause in some cases.

G. Para 17.1 of the National Policy shows that the policy aims at implementation of International obligations/commitments in all sectors on the empowerment of women such as the CEDAW etc. As regards the implementation of the International Instruments, it has already been stated that the Supreme Court has, in the absence of legislation under Article 253 of the Constitution, viewed that Courts are under an obligation to give due regard to the International Conventions and norms for construing domestic laws, more so, when there is no inconsistency between them (international instruments and domestic laws) and there is a void in domestic laws; and that International Covenants and declarations are to be respected by all signatories.

H. The CEDAW provides : "To prohibit, subject to the imposition of sanctions, dismissal on the **grounds of pregnancy** or maternity leave and discrimination in dismissal on the basis of **marital status"** [see Article 11(2) (a)]. In this regard, the Supreme Court has held that Regulations/ Rules denying the right to employment to a married women and that providing pregnancy as a bar to continue in service of Air Hostess are ultra vires of the Constitution (see Chapter two). There may be such Regulations or Rules in other undertakings of the Governments and private undertakings which are required to be made out-dated.

I. The question of "rape" is a serious question. The history of mankind tells us about commission of rape, including marital rape, and rape amongst the farmers. It is because of the fact that men have stronger sexual feelings than women. It cannot be totally eradicated for varieties of factors such as gundaism, armed conflicts etc. Murderers are hanged till death, yet murderer is every where. The law relating to rape should be reviewed suitably in the light of the international instruments, including protective measures.

J Prostitutes may be of either sex, i.e. heterosexual or homosexual activity. Most of the English Dictionaries have defined "prostitute" to mean a person who offers herself/himself for sexual intercourse for money or other valuables, whereas some other dictionaries say that woman who offers her body to discriminate sexual intercourse for hire, say, the *Concise Oxford Dictionary*. But historically the prostitution relates to woman who earns money by having sex with man. The National Policy also refers to female prostitutes. Therefore, the expression "prostitute", in the context, is referred to a woman who offers her body to indiscriminate sexual intercourse for money or other valuables, and such a woman may answer the description of a public prostitute, as distinct from kept-woman who is not available for sexual relationship with others.

Prostitution is a very old and universal phenomenon. In some countries, prostitutes were required distinctive dress; in some countries, they were required to live in a special area of a town or city, otherwise known as the "red-light district"; and in some countries, prostitutions were licensed and regulated by laws. However, in the 16th century brothels were to be closed in some countries because of epidemic of venereal disease. Some countries have banned prostitution. In 1949, the UN General Assembly adopted a convention for the suppression of prostitution. It may be stated that prostitution is largely responsible for the spread of AIDS and for orphaning of thousands of children. The effect of the AIDS/HIV virus is known to everywhere in the world. As regards girl children born to prostitutes, they are trained up for prostitution. Some of the girls who refuse the same become mentally sick. I have seen one or two such children in the Rehabititation Centre of SEVAC in Kolkota. Therefore, the appropriate government has to make a policy for the care of the offsprings of prostitutes and to make them a part of the society.

The main cause of the prostitution is poverty. Therefore, unless the economy of women is improved, the total suppression of prostitution may not be possible.

K. Again, law is not sufficient to fight the evils of gender bias. Individuals and their community should also contribute to the full enjoyment of women's right and not to place or put obstacles in the process. As stated, systematic discussion on "of gender bias" is very essential as it would have a tremendous effect on the people and it will make to devise scheme as to meet the realities in life and human rights education. The media, namely TV, should be made to involve in the matters of publicity by way of play or serials or otherwise towards the goals of gender equality. The "Institutional Mechanisms" provided under the National Policy should not be only on paper.

Appendix – I

UNIVERSAL DECLARATION OF HUMAN RIGHTS

(Adopted by the General Assembly of the United Nations on 10 December 1948)

Preamble

Whereas recognition of the inherent dignity and of the equal and inalienable rights of all members of the human family is the foundation of freedom, justice and peace in the world,

Whereas disregard and contempt for human rights have resulted in barbarous acts which have outraged the conscience of mankind, and the advent of a world in which human beings shall enjoy freedom of speech and belief and freedom from fear and want has been proclaimed as the highest aspiration of the common people,

Whereas it is essential, if man is not to be compelled to have recourse, as a last resort, to rebellion against tyranny and oppression, that human rights should be protected by the rule of law,

Whereas it is essential to promote the development of friendly relations between nations,

Whereas the peoples of the United Nations have in the Charter reaffirmed their faith in fundamental human rights, in the dignity and worth of the human person and in the equal rights of men and women and have determined to promote social progress and better standards of life in larger freedom,

Whereas Member States have pledged themselves to achieve, in co-operation with the United Nations, the promotion of universal respect for and observance of human rights and fundamental freedoms,

Whereas a common understanding of these rights and freedoms is of the greatest importance for the full realization of this pledge,

Now, therefore, THE GENERAL ASSEMBLY proclaims

THIS UNIVERSAL DECLARATION OF HUMAN RIGHTS as a common standard of achievement for all peoples and all nations, to the end that every individual and every organ of society, keeping this Declaration constantly in mind, shall strive by teaching and education to promote respect for these rights and freedoms and by progressive measures, national and international, to secure their universal and effective recognition and observance, both among the peoples of Member States themselves and among the peoples of territories under their jurisdiction.

Article 1

All human beings are born free and equal in

dignity and rights. They are endowed with reason and conscience and should act towards one another in a spirit of brotherhood.

Article 2

Everyone is entitled to all the rights and freedoms set forth in this Declaration, without distinction of any kind, such as race, colour, sex, language, religion, political or other opinion, national or social origin, property, birth or other status.

Furthermore, no distinction shall be made on the basis of the political, jurisdictional or international status of the country or territory to which a person belongs, whether it be independent, trust, non-self-governing or under any other limitation of sovereignty.

Article 3

Everyone has the right to life, liberty and security of person.

Article 4

No one shall be held in slavery or servitude; slavery and the slave trade shall be prohibited in all their forms.

Article 5

No one shall be subjected to torture or to cruel, inhuman or degrading treatment or punishment.

Article 6

Everyone has the right to recognition everywhere as a person before the law.

Article 7

All are equal before the law and are entitled without any discrimination to equal protection of the law. All are entitled to equal protection against any discrimination in violation of this Declaration and against any incitement to such discrimination.

Article 8

Everyone has the right to an effective remedy by the competent national tribunals for acts violating the fundamental rights granted him by the constitution or by law.

Article 9

No one shall be subjected to arbitrary arrest, detention or exile.

Article 10

Everyone is entitled in full equality to a fair and public hearing by an independent and impartial tribunal, in the determination of his rights and obligations and of any criminal charge against him.

Article 11

(1) Everyone charged with a penal offence has the right to be presumed innocent until proved guilty according to law in a public trial at which he has had all the guarantees necessary for his defence.

(2) No one shall be held guilty of any penal offence on account of any act or omission which did not constitute a penal offence, under national or international law, at the time when it was

committed. Nor shall a heavier penalty be imposed than the one that was applicable at the time the penal offence was committed.

Article 12

No one shall be subjected to arbitrary interference with his privacy, family, home or correspondence, nor to attacks upon his honour and reputation. Everyone has the right to the protection of the law against such interference or attacks.

Article 13

(1) Everyone has the right to freedom of movement and residence within the borders of each state.

(2) Everyone has the right to leave any country, including his own, and to return to his country.

Article 14

(1) Everyone has the right to seek and to enjoy in other countries asylum from persecution.

(2) This right may not be invoked in the case of prosecutions genuinely arising from non-political crimes or from acts contrary to the purposes and principles of the United Nations.

Article 15

(1) Everyone has the right to a nationality.

(2) No one shall be arbitrarily deprived of his nationality nor denied the right to change his nationality.

Article 16

(1) Men and women of full age, without any limitation due to race, nationality or religion, have the right to marry and to found a family. They are entitled to equal rights as to marriage, during marriage and at its dissolution.

(2) Marriage shall be entered into only with the free and full consent of the intending spouses.

(3) The family is the natural and fundamental group unit of society and is entitled to protection by society and the State.

Article 17

(1) Everyone has the right to own property alone as well as in association with others.

(2) No one shall be arbitrarily deprived of his property.

Article 18

Everyone has the right to freedom of thought, conscience and religion; this right includes freedom to change his religion or belief, and freedom, either alone or in community with others and in public or private, to manifest his religion or belief in teaching, practice, worship and observance.

Article 19

Everyone has the right to freedom of opinion and expression; this right includes freedom to hold opinions without interference and to seek, receive and impart information and ideas through any media and regardless of frontiers.

Article 20

(1) Everyone has the right to freedom of peaceful assembly and association.

(2) No one may be compelled to belong to an association.

Article 21

(1) Everyone has the right to take part in the government of his country, directly or through freely chosen representatives.

(2) Everyone has the right to equal access to public service in his country.

(3) The will of the people shall be the basis of the authority of government; this shall be expressed in periodic and genuine elections which shall be by universal and equal suffrage and shall be held by secret vote or by equivalent free voting procedures.

Article 22

Everyone, as a member of society, has the right to social security and is entitled to realization, through national effort and international co-operation and in accordance with the organization and resources of each State, of the economic, social and cultural rights indispensable for his dignity and the free development of his personality.

Article 23

(1) Everyone has the right to work, to free choice of

employment, to just and favourable conditions of work and to protection against unemployment.

(2) Everyone, without any discrimination, has the right to equal pay for equal work.

(3) Everyone who works has the right to just and favourable remuneration ensuring for himself and his family an existence worthy of human dignity, and supplemented, if necessary, by other means of social protection.

(4) Everyone has the right to form and to join trade unions for the protection of his interests.

Article 24

Everyone has the right to rest and leisure, including reasonable limitation of working hours and periodic holidays with pay.

Article 25

(1) Everyone has the right to a standard of living adequate for the health and well-being of himself and of his family, including food, clothing, housing and medical care and necessary social services, and the right to security in the event of unemployment, sickness, disability, widowhood, old age or other lack of livelihood in circumstances beyond his control.

(2) Motherhood and childhood are entitled to special care and assistance. All children, whether born in or out of wedlock, shall enjoy the same social protection.

Article 26

(1) Everyone has the right to education. Education shall be free, at least in the elementary and fundamental stages. Elementary education shall be compulsory. Technical and professional education shall be made generally available and higher education shall be equally accessible to all on the basis of merit.

(2) Education shall be directed to the full development of the human personality and to the strengthening of respect for human rights and fundamental freedoms. It shall promote understanding, tolerance and friendship among all nations, racial or religious groups, and shall further the activities of the United Nations for the maintenance of peace.

(3) Parents have a prior right to choose the kind of education that shall be given to their children.

Article 27

(1) Everyone has the right freely to participate in the cultural life of the community, to enjoy the arts and to share in scientific advancement and its benefits.

(2) Everyone has the right to the protection of the moral and material interests resulting from any scientific, literary or artistic production of which he is the author.

Article 28

Everyone is entitled to a social and international

order in which the rights and freedoms set forth in this Declaration can be fully realized.

Article 29

(1) Everyone has duties to the community in which alone the free and full development of his personality is possible.

(2) In the exercise of his rights and freedoms, everyone shall be subject only to such limitations as are determined by law solely for the purpose of securing due recognition and respect for the rights and freedoms of others and of meeting the just requirements of morality, public order and the general welfare in a democratic society.

(3) These rights and freedoms may in no case be exercised contrary to the purposes and principles of the United Nations.

Article 30

Nothing in this Declaration may be interpreted as implying for any State, group or person any right to engage in any activity or to perform any act aimed at the destruction of any of the rights and freedoms set forth herein.

Appendix - II

CONVENTION ON THE ELIMINATION OF ALL FORMS OF DISCRIMINATION AGAINST WOMEN- 1979

The full text of the Convention is set out below after omitting the preliminary or introduction

PART I

Article 1

For the purposes of the present Convention, the term "discrimination against women" shall mean any distinction, exclusion or restriction made on the basis of sex which has the effect or purpose of impairing or nullifying the recognition, enjoyment or exercise by women, irrespective of their marital status, on a basis of equality of men and women, of human rights and fundamental freedom in the political, economic, social, cultural, civil or any other field.

Article 2

States Parties condemn discrimination against

women in all its forms, agree to pursue by all appropriate means and without delay a policy of eliminating discrimination against women and, to this end, undertake:

(a) To embody the principle of the equality of men and women in their national constitutions or other appropriate legislation if not yet incorporated therein and to ensure, through law and other appropriate means, the practical realisation of this principle;

(b) To adopt appropriate legislative and other measures, including sanctions where appropriate, prohibiting all discrimination against women;

(c) To establish legal protection of the rights of women on an equal basis with men and to ensure through competent national tribunals and other public institutions the effective protective of women against any act of discrimination;

(d) To refrain from engaging in any act or practice of discrimination against women and to ensure that public authorities and institutions shall act in conformity with this obligation;

(e) To take all appropriate measures to eliminate discrimination against women by any person, organisation or enterprise;

(f) To take all appropriate measures, including legislation, to modify or abolish existing laws, regulations, customs and practices which constitute discrimination against women;

(g) To repeal all national penal provisions which constitute discrimination against women;

Article 3

States Parties shall take in all fields, in particular in the political, social, economic and cultural fields, all appropriate measures, including legislation, to ensure the full development and advancement of women, for the purpose of guaranteeing them the exercise and enjoyment of human rights and fundamental freedom on a basis of equality with men.

Article 4

1. Adoption by States Parties of temporary special measures aimed at accelerating de facto equality between men and women shall not be considered discrimination as defined in the present Convention, but shall in no way entail as a consequence the maintenance of unequal or separate standards; these measures shall be discontinued when the objectives of equality of opportunity and treatment have been achieved.
2. Adoption by States Parties of special measures, including those measures contained in the present Convention, aimed at protecting maternity shall not be considered discriminatory.

Article 5

States Parties shall take all appropriate measures:

a) To modify the social and cultural patterns of conduct of men and women, with a view to achieving the elimination of prejudices and customary and all other practices which are based on the idea of the inferiority or the superiority of either of the sexes or on stereotyped roles for men and women;

b) To ensure that family education includes a proper understanding of maternity as a social function and the recognition of the common responsibility of men and women in the upbringing and development of their children, it being understood that the interest of the children is the primordial consideration in all cases.

Article 6

States Parties shall take all appropriate measures, including legislation, to suppress all forms of traffic in women and exploitation of prostitution of women.

PART II

Article 7

States Parties shall take all appropriate measures to eliminate discrimination against women in the political and public life of the country and, in particular, shall ensure to women, on equal terms with men, the rights:

(a) To vote in all elections and public referenda and to be eligible for election to all publicly elected bodies;

(b) To participate in the formulation of government policy and the implementation thereof to hold public office and perform all public functions at all levels of government;

(c) To participate in non-government organisation and associations concerned with the public and political life of the country.

Article 8

States Parties shall take all appropriate measures to ensure to women, on equal terms with men and without any discrimination, the opportunity to represent their governments at the international level and to participate in the work of international organizations.

Article 9

1. States Parties shall grant women equal rights with men to acquire, change or retain their nationality. They shall ensure in particular that neither marriage to an alien nor change of nationality by the husband during marriage shall automatically change the nationality of the wife, render her stateless or force upon her the nationality of the husband.
2. States Parties shall grant women equal rights with men with respect to the nationality of their children.

Part III

Article 10

States parties shall take all appropriate measures to eliminate discrimination against women in order to ensure to them equal rights with men in the field of education and in particular to ensure, on a basis of equality of men and women:

(a) The same conditions for career and vocational guidance, for access to studies and for the achievement of diplomas in educational establishments of all categories in rural as well as in urban areas; this equality shall be ensured in pre-school, general, technical, professional and higher technical education, as well as in all types of vocational training;

(b) Access to the same curricula, the same examinations, teaching staff with qualifications of the same standard and school premises and equipment of the same quality;

(c) The elimination of any stereotyped concept of the roles of men at all levels and in all forms of education by encouraging co-education and other types of education which will help to achieve this aim and in particular, by the revision of textbooks and school programmes and the adaptation of teaching methods:

(d) The same opportunities to benefit from scholarships and other study grants;

(e) The same opportunities for access to programmes of continuing education including adult and functional literacy programmes, particularly those aimed at reducing, at the earliest possible time, any gap in education existing between men and women;

(f) The reduction of female student drop-out rates and the organisation of programmes for girls and women who have left school prematurely;

(g) The same opportunities to participate actively in sports and physical education;

(h) Access to specific educational information to help to ensure the health and well-being of families, including information and advice on family planning.

Article 11

1. States parties shall take all appropriate measures to eliminate discrimination against women in the field of employment in order to ensure, on a basis of equality of men and women, the same rights, in particular:

(a) The right to work as an inalienable right of all human beings;

(b) The right to the same employment opportunities including the application of the same criteria for selection in matters of employment;

(c) The right to free choice of profession and employment, the right to promotion, job security and all benefits and conditions of service and the right to receive vocational training and retraining, including apprenticeship, advanced vocational training and recurrent training.

(d) The right to equal remuneration, including benefits, and to equal treatment in respect of work of equal value, as well as equality of treatment in the evaluation of the quality of work;

(e) The right to social security, particularly in cases of retirement, unemployment, sickness, invalidity and old age and other incapacity to work, as well as the right to paid leave;

(f) The right to protection of health and to safety in working conditions, including the safeguarding of the function of reproduction.

2. In order to prevent discrimination against women on the grounds of marriage or maternity and to ensure their effective right to work, States Parties shall take appropriate measure;

(a) To prohibit, subject to the imposition of sanctions, dismissal on the grounds of pregnancy or maternity leave and discrimination in dismissals on the basis of marital status;

(b) To introduce maternity leave with pay or with comparable social benefits without loss of former employment, seniority or social allowance;

(c) To encourage the provisions of the necessary supporting social services to enable parents to combine family obligations with work responsibilities and participants in public life, in particular through promoting the establishment and development of a network of child-care facilities;

(d) To provide special protection to women during pregnancy in types of work proved to be harmful to them.

3. Protective legislation relating to matters covered in this article shall be reviewed periodically in the light of scientific and technological knowledge and shall be revised, repealed or extended as necessary.

Article 12

1. States Parties shall take all appropriate measures to eliminate discrimination against women in the field of health care in order to ensure, on a basis of equality of men and women, access to health care services, including those related to family planning.

2. Notwithstanding the provisions of paragraph 1 of this article, States Parties shall ensure to women appropriate services in connection with pregnancy, confinement and the post-natal period, granting free services where necessary, as well as adequate nutrition during pregnancy and lactation.

Article 13

1. States Parties shall take all appropriate measures to eliminate discrimination against women in other areas of economic and social life in order to ensure, on a basis of equality of men and women, the same rights, in particular:

(a) The right to family benefits;

(b) The right to bank loans, mortgages and other forms of financial credit;

(c) The right to participate in recreational activities, sports and all aspects of cultural life.

Article 14

1. States Parties shall take into account the particular problems faced by rural women and the significant roles which rural women play in the economic survival of their families, including their work in the non-monetized sectors of the economy, and shall take all appropriate measure to ensure the application of the provisions of this Convention to women in rural areas.

2. States Parties shall take all appropriate measures to eliminate discrimination against women in rural areas in order to ensure, on a basis of equality of men and women, that they participate in and benefit from rural development and in particular, shall ensure to such women the right:

   (a) To participate in the elaboration and implementation of development planning at all levels;

   (b) To have access to adequate health care facilities, including information, counseling and services in family planning;

   (c) To benefit directly from social security programmes;

(d) To obtain all types of training and education, formal and non-formal, including that relating to functional literacy, as well as, inter alia, the benefit of all community and extension services, in order to increase their technical proficiency;

(e) To organize self-help groups and cooperatives in order to obtain equal access to economic opportunities through employment or self-employment;

(f) To participate in all community activities;

(g) To have access to agricultural credit and loans, marketing facilities, appropriate technology and equal treatment in land and agrarian reform as well as in land resettlement schemes;

(h) To enjoy adequate living conditions, particularly in relation to housing, sanitation, electricity and water supply, transport and communications.

PART IV

Article 15

(1) States Parties shall accord to women equality with men before the law.

(2) States Parties shall accord to women, in civil matters, a legal capacity identical to that of men and the same opportunities to exercise that capacity. In particular, they shall give women

equal rights to conclude contracts and to administer property and shall treat them equally in all stages of procedures in courts and tribunals.

(3) States Parties agree that all contracts and all other private instruments of any kind with a legal effect which is directed at restricting the legal capacity of women shall be deemed null and void.

(4) Sates Parties shall accord to men and women the same rights with regard to the laws relating to the movement of persons and the freedom to choose their residence and domicile.

Article 16

1. States Parties shall take all appropriate measures to eliminate discrimination against women in all matters relating to marriage and family relations and in particular shall ensure, on a basis of equality of men and women:

   (a) The same right to enter into marriage;

   (b) The same right freely to choose a spouse and to enter into marriage only with their free and full consent;

   (c) The same rights and responsibilities during marriage and at its dissolution;

   (d) The same rights and responsibilities as parents, irrespective of their marital status, in matter relating to their children; in all cases the interests of the children shall be paramount;

(e) The same right to decide freely and responsibly on the number and spacing of their children and to have access to the information, education and means to enable them to exercise these rights;

(f) The same rights and responsibilities with regard to guardianship, wardship, trusteeship and adoption of children, or similar institutions where these concepts exist in national legislation, in all cases the interests of the children shall be paramount;

(g) The same personal rights as husband and wife, including the right to choose a family name, a profession and an occupation;

(h) The same rights for both spouses in respect of the ownership, acquisition, management, administration, enjoyment and disposition of property, whether free of charge or for a valuable consideration.

2. The betrothal and the marriage of a child shall have no legal effect, and all necessary action including legislation, shall be taken to specify a minimum age for marriage and to make the registration of marriages in an official registry compulsory.

PART V

Article 17

1. For the purpose of considering the progress made in the implementation of the present Convention,

there shall be established a Committee on the Elimination of Discrimination against Women (hereinafter referred to as the Committee) consisting, at the time of entry into force of the Convention, of eighteen and after ratification of or accession to the Convention by the thirty-fifth State Party of twenty-three experts of high moral standing and competence in the field covered by the Convention. The experts shall be elected by States Parties from among their national and shall serve in their personal capacity consideration being given to equitable geographical distribution and to the representation of the different forms of civilization as well as the principle legal systems.

2. The members of the Committee shall be elected by secret ballot from a list of persons nominated by States Parties. Each State Party may nominate one person from among its own nationals.

3. The initial election shall be held six months after the date of the entry into force of the present Convention. At least three months before the date of each election the Secretary-General of the United Nations shall address a letter to the States Parties inviting them to submit their nominations within two months. The Secretary-General shall prepare a list in alphabetical order of all persons thus nominated, indicating the States Parties which have nominated them, and shall submit it to the States Parties.

4. Elections of the members of the Committee shall be held at a meeting of States Parties convened by

the Secretary-General at United Nations Headquarters. At that meeting, for which two thirds of the States Parties shall constitute a quorum, the persons elected to the committee shall be those nominees who obtain the largest number of votes and an absolute majority of the votes of the representatives of States Parties present and voting.

5. The members of the Committee shall be elected for a term of four years. However, the terms of nine of the members elected at the first election shall expire at the end of two years; immediately after the first election the names of these nine members shall be chosen by lot by the Chairman of the Committee.

6. The election of the five additional members of the Committee shall be held in accordance with the provisions of paragraphs 2,3, and 4 of this article, following the thirty-fifth ratification or accession. The terms of two of the additional members elected on this occasion shall expire at the end of two years, the names of these two members having been chosen by lot by the Chairman of the Committee.

7. For the filing of casual vacancies, the State Party whose expert has ceased to function as a member of the Committee shall appoint another expert from among its nationals, subject to the approval of the Committee.

8. The members of the Committee shall, with the approval of the General Assembly, receive

emoluments from United Nations resources on such terms and conditions as the Assembly may decide, having regard to the importance of the Committee's responsibilities.

9. The Secretary-General of the United Nations shall provide the necessary staff and facilities for the effective performance of the functions of the Committee under the present convention.

Article 18

1 States Parties undertake to submit to the Secretary-General of the United Nations for consideration by the Committee, a report on the legislative, judicial, administrative or other measures which they have adopted to give effect to the provisions of the present Convention and on the progress made in this respect:

   (a) Within a year after the entry into force for the State concerned; and

   (b) Thereafter at least every four years and further whenever the Committee so requests.

2. Reports may indicate factors and difficulties affecting the degree of fulfillment of obligations under the present Convention.

Article 19

1. The Committee shall adopt its own rules of procedure.

2. The Committee shall elect its officers for a term of two years.

Article 20

1. The Committee shall normally meet for a period of not more than two weeks annually in order to consider the reports submitted in accordance with article 18 of the present Convention.

2. The meetings of the Committee shall normally be held at United Nations headquarters or at any other convenient place as determined by the Committee

Article 21

1. The Committee shall, through the Economic and Social Council, report annually to the General Assembly of the United Nations on its activities and may make suggestions and general recommendations based on the examination of reports and information received from the States Parties. Such suggestions and general recommendations shall be included in the report of the Committee together with comments, if any, from States Parties.

2. The Secretary-General shall transmit the reports of the Committee to the Commission on the Status of Women for its information.

Article 22

The specialised agencies shall be entitled to be represented at the consideration of the implementation of such provisions of the present Convention as fall within the scope of their activities. The Committee may invite the specialised agencies to submit reports on the implementation of the Convention in areas falling within the scope of their activities.

PART VI

Article 23

Nothing in this Convention shall affect any provisions that are more conductive to the achievement of equality between men and women which may be contained:

(a) In the legislation of a State Party; or

(b) In any other international convention, treaty or agreement in force for that State.

Article 24

States Parties undertake to adopt all necessary measures at the national level aimed at achieving the full realisation of the rights recognised in the present Convention.

Article 25

(1) The present Convention shall be open for signature by all States.

(2) The Secretary-General of the United Nations is designated as the depository of the present Convention.

(3) The present Convention is subject to ratification. Instruments of ratification shall be deposited with the Secretary-General of the United nations.

(4) The present Convention shall be open to accession

by all States. Accession shall be effected by the deposit of an instrument of accession with the Secretary -General of the United Nations.

Article 26

(1) A request for the revision of the present Convention may be made at any time by any State Party by means of a notification in writing addressed to the Secretary-General of the United Nations.

(2) The General Assembly of the United Nations shall decide upon the steps, if any, to be taken in respect of such a request.

Article 27

(1) The present Convention shall enter into force on the thirtieth day after the date of deposit with the Secretary-General of the United Nations of the twentieth instrument of ratification or accession.

(2) For each State ratifying the present Convention or acceding to it after the deposit of the twentieth instrument of ratification or accession, the Convention shall enter into force on the thirtieth day after the date of the deposit of its own instrument of ratification or accession.

Article 28

(1) The Secretary-General of the United Nations shall receive and circulate to all States the text of reservations made by States at the time of ratification or accession.

(2) A reservation incompatible with the object and purpose of the present Convention shall not be permitted.

(3) Reservations may be withdrawn at any time by notification to this effect addressed to the Secretary-General of the United Nations, who shall then inform all States thereof. Such notification shall take effect on the date on which it is received.

Article 29

1. Any dispute between two or more States Parties concerning the interpretation or application of the present Convention which is not settled by negotiation shall, at the request of one of them, be submitted to arbitration. If within six months from the date of the request for arbitration the parties are unable to agree on the organisation of the arbitration, anyone of those parties may refer the dispute to the International Court of Justice by request in conformity with the Statute of the Court.

2. Each State Party may at time of signature or ratification of this Convention or accession thereto declare that it does not consider itself bound by paragraph 1 of this article. The other State Parties shall not be bound by that paragraph with respect to any State Party which has made such a reservation.

3. Any State Party which has made a reservation in accordance with paragraph 2 of this article may at

any time withdraw that reservation by notification to the Secretary General of the United Nations.

Article 30

The present Convention, the Arabic, Chinese, English, French, Russian and Spanish texts of which are equally authentic, shall be deposited with the Secretary-General of the United Nations.

Appendix- III

NATIONAL POLICY FOR THE EMPOWERMENT OF WOMEN, 2001 DEPARTMENT OF WOMEN & CHILD DEVELOPMENT MINISTRY OF HUMAN RESOURCE DEVELOPMENT GOVERNMENT OF INDIA

Contents

Introduction

1.1 The principle of gender equality is enshrined in the Indian Constitution in its Preamble, Fundamental Rights, Fundamental Duties and Directive Principles. The Constitution not only grants equality to women, but also empowers the State to adopt measures of positive discrimination in favour of women.

1.2 Within the framework of a democratic polity, our laws, development policies, plans and programmes have aimed at women's advancement in different spheres. From the Fifth Five Year Plan (1974-78) onwards, there has been a marked shift in the approach to women's issues from welfare to development. In recent years, the empowerment of women has been recognised as a central issue in determining the status of women. The National Commission for Women was set up by an Act of Parliament in 1990 to safeguard the rights and legal entitlements of women. The 73rd and 74th Amendments (1993) to the Constitution of India have provided for reservation of seats in the local bodies of Panchayats and Municipalities for women, laying a strong foundation for their participation in decision making at the local levels.

1.3 India has also ratified various international conventions and human rights instruments committing to secure equal rights of women. Key among them is the ratification of the Convention on Elimination of All Forms of Discrimination against Women (CEDAW) in 1993.

1.4 The Mexico Plan of Action (1975), the Nairobi Forward Looking Strategies (1985), the Beijing Declaration as well as the Platform for Action (1995) and the Outcome Document adopted by the UNGA Session on Gender Equality and

Development & Peace for the 21st century, titled "Further actions and initiatives to implement the Beijing Declaration and the Platform for Action" have been unreservedly endorsed by India for appropriate follow up.

1.5 The Policy also takes note of the commitments of the Ninth Five Year plan and the other Sectoral Policies relating to empowerment of women.

1.6 The women's movement and a wide-spread network of non-government organisations which have strong grassroots presence and deep insight into women's concerns have contributed in inspiring women's concerns initiatives for the empowerment of women.

1.7 However, there still exists a wide gap between the goals enunciated in the Constitution, legislation, policies, plans, programmes, and related mechanisms on the one hand and the situational reality of the status of women in India, on the other. This has been analysed extensively in the Report of the Committee on the Status of Women in India, "Towards Equality", 1974 and high lighted in the National Perspective Plan for Women, 1988-2000, the Shramshakti Report, 1988 and the "Platform for Action, Five Years after - An Assessment".

1.8 Gender disparity manifests itself in various forms, the most obvious being the trend of continuously declining female ratio in the population in the last few decades. Social stereotyping and violence at the domestic and societal levels are some of the other manifestations. Discrimination against girl children, adolescent girls and women persists in parts of the country.

1.9 The underlying causes of gender inequality are related to social and economic structure, which is based on informal and formal norms, and practices.

1.10 Consequently, the access of women particularly those belonging to weaker sections including Scheduled Castes/Scheduled Tribes/ Other Backward Classes and minorities, majority of whom are in the rural areas and in the informal, unorganised sector - to education, health and productive resources, among others, is inadequate. Therefore, they remain largely marginalised, poor and socially excluded.

Goals and Objectives

1.11 The goal of this Policy is to bring about the advancement, development and empowerment of women. The Policy will be widely disseminated so as to encourage active participation of all stakeholders for achieving its goals. Specifically, the objectives of this Policy include:

(i) Creating an environment through positive economic and social policies for full development of women to enable them to realise their full potential;

(ii) The de-jure and de-facto enjoyment of all human rights and fundamental freedom by women on equal basis with men in all spheres - political, economic, social, cultural and civil;

(iii) Equal access to participation and decision-making of women in social, political and economic life of the nation;

(iv) Equal access to women to health care, quality education at all levels, career and vocational guidance, employment, equal remuneration, occupational health and safety, social security and public office etc;

(v) Strengthening legal systems aimed at elimination of all forms of discrimination against women;

(vi) Changing societal attitudes and community practices by active participation and involvement of both men and women;

(vii) Mainstreaming a gender perspective in the development process;

(viii) Elimination of discrimination and all forms of violence against women and the girl child; and

(ix) Building and strengthening partnerships with civil society, particularly women's organisations.

Policy Prescriptions

Judicial Legal Systems

2.1 Legal-judicial system will be made more responsive and gender sensitive to women's needs, especially in cases of domestic violence and personal assault. New laws will be enacted and existing laws reviewed to ensure that justice is quick and the punishment meted out to the culprits is commensurate with the severity of the offence.

2.2 At the initiative of and with the full participation of all stakeholders including community and religious leaders, the Policy would aim to encourage changes in personal laws such as those related to marriage, divorce, maintenance and guardianship so as to eliminate discrimination against women.

2.3 The evolution of property rights in a patriarchal system has contributed to the subordinate status of women. The policy would aim to encourage change in laws relating to ownership of property and inheritance by evolving consensus in order to make them gender just.

Decision-making

3.1 Women's equality in power sharing and active participation in decision-making, including decision-making in political process at all levels will be ensured for the achievement of the goals of empowerment. All measures will be taken to guarantee women equal access to and full participation in decision-making bodies at every level, including the legislative, executive, judicial, corporate, statutory bodies, as also the advisory Commissions, Committees, Boards, Trusts etc. Affirmative action such as reservations/quotas, including in higher legislative bodies, will be considered whenever necessary on a time bound basis. Women-friendly personnel policies will also be drawn up to encourage women to participate effectively in the developmental process.

Mainstreaming a Gender Perspective in the Development Process

4.1 Policies, programmes and systems will be established to ensure mainstreaming of women's perspectives in all developmental processes, as catalysts, participants and recipients. Wherever there are gaps in policies and programmes, women specific interventions would be undertaken to bridge these. Coordinating and monitoring mechanisms will also be devised to assess from time to time the progress of such mainstreaming mechanisms. Women's issues and concerns as a result will specially be addressed and reflected in all concerned laws, sectoral policies, plans and programmes of action.

Economic Empowerment of Women
Poverty Eradication

5.1 Since women comprise the majority of the population below the poverty line and are very often in situations of extreme poverty, given the harsh realities of intra-household and social discrimination, macroeconomic policies and poverty eradication programmes will specifically address the needs and problems of such women. There will be improved implementation of programmes which are already women oriented with special targets for women. Steps will be taken for mobilisation of poor women and convergence of services, by offering them a range of economic and social options, along with necessary support measures to enhance their capabilities.

Micro-Credit

5.2 In order to enhance women's access to credit for consumption and production, the establishment of new, and strengthening of existing micro-credit mechanisms and micro-finance institutions will be undertaken so that the outreach of credit is enhanced. Other supportive measures would be taken to ensure adequate flow of credit through extant financial institutions and banks, so that all women below poverty line have easy access to credit.

Women and Economy

5.3 Women's perspectives will be included in designing and implementing macroeconomic and social policies by institutionalising their participation in such processes. Their contribution to socio-economic development as producers and workers will be recognised in the formal and informal sectors (including home based workers) and appropriate policies relating to employment and to her working conditions will be drawn up. Such measures could include:

(a) Reinterpretation and redefinition of conventional concepts of work wherever necessary, eg in the Census records, to reflect women's contribution as producers and workers.

(b) Preparation of satellite and national accounts.

(c) Development of appropriate methodologies for undertaking (a) and (b) above.

Globalisation

5.4 Globalisation has presented new challenges for the realisation of the goal of women's equality, the gender impact of which has not been systematically evaluated fully. However, from the micro-level studies that were commissioned by the Department of Women & Child Development, it is evident that there is a need for re-framing policies for access to employment and quality of employment. Benefits of the growing global economy have been unevenly distributed leading to wider economic disparities, the feminisation of poverty, increased gender inequality through often deteriorating working conditions and unsafe working environment especially in the informal economy and rural areas. Strategies will be designed to enhance the capacity of women and empower them to meet the negative social and economic impacts, which may flow from the globalisation process.

Women and Agriculture

5.5 In view of the critical role of women in the agriculture and allied sectors, as producers, concentrated efforts will be made to ensure that benefits of training, extension and various programmes will reach them in proportion to their numbers. The programmes for training women in soil conservation, social forestry, dairy development and other occupations allied to agriculture like horticulture, livestock including small animal husbandry, poultry, fisheries etc, will be expanded to benefit women workers in the agriculture sector.

Women of industry

5.6 The important role played by women in electronics, information technology and food processing and agro industry and textiles has been crucial to the development of these sectors. They would be given comprehensive support in terms of labour legislation, social security and other support services to participate in various industrial sectors.

5.7 Women at present cannot work in night shift in factories even if they wish to. Suitable measures will be taken to enable women to work in night shift in factories. This will be accompanied with support services for security transportation etc.

Support Services

5.8 The provision of support services for women, like child care facilities, creches at work places and educational institutions, homes for the aged and the disabled will be expanded and improved to create an enabling environment and to ensure their full cooperation in social, political and economic life. Women-friendly personnel policies will also be drawn up to encourage women to participate effectively in the developmental process.

Social Empowerment of Women

Education

6.1 Equal access to education for women and girls will be ensured. Special measures will be taken to eliminate discrimination, universalise education, eradicate illiteracy, create a gender sensitive educational system, increase enrolment and retention rates of girls and improve the quality of education to facilitate life-long learning as well as development of vocational/technical skills by women. Reducing the gender gap in secondary and higher education would be a focus area.

Sectoral time targets in existing policies will be achieved, with a special focus on girls and women, particularly those belonging to weaker sections including the Scheduled Castes/Scheduled Tribes/ Other Backward Classes/Minorities. Gender sensitive curricula would be developed at all levels of educational system in order to address sex stereotyping as one of the causes of gender discrimination.

Health

6.2 A holistic approach to women's health which includes both nutrition and health services will be adopted and special attention will be given to the needs of women and the girl at all stages of the life cycle. The reduction of infant mortality and maternal mortality, which are sensitive indicators of human development, is a priority concern. This policy reiterates the national demographic goals for Infant Mortality Rate (IMR), Maternal Mortality Rate (MMR) that are set out in the National Population Policy 2000. Women should have access to comprehensive, affordable and quality health care. Measures will be adopted that take into account the reproductive rights of women to enable them to exercise informed choices, their vulnerability to sexual and health problems together with endemic, infectious and communicable diseases such as malaria, TB, and water borne diseases as well as hypertension and cardio-pulmonary diseases. The social, developmental and health consequences of HIV/AIDS and other sexually transmitted diseases will be tackled from a gender perspective.

6.3 To effectively meet problems of infant and maternal mortality, and early marriage, the availability of good and accurate data at microlevel on deaths, birth and marriages is required. Strict implementation of registration of births and deaths would be ensured and registration of marriages would be made compulsory.

6.4 In accordance with the commitment of the National Population Policy (2000) to population stabilisation, the Policy recognises the critical need of men and women to have access to safe, effective and affordable methods of family planning of their choice and the need to suitably address the issues of early marriages and spacing of children. Interventions such as spread of education, compulsory registration of marriage and special programmes like Balika Samridhi Yojana should impact on delaying the age of marriage so that by 2010 child marriages are eliminated.

6.5 Women's traditional knowledge about health care and nutrition will be recognised through proper documentation and its use will be encouraged. The use of Indian and alternative systems of medicine will be enhanced within the framework of overall health infrastructure available for women.

Nutrition

6.6 In view of the high risk of malnutrition and disease that women face at all the three critical stages viz. infancy and childhood, adolescent and reproductive phase, focussed attention would be paid to meeting the nutritional needs of women at all stages of the life cycle. This is also important in view of the critical link between the health of adolescent girls, pregnant and lactating women with the health of infant and young children. Special efforts will be made to tackle the problem of macro and micro nutrient deficiencies especially amongst pregnant and lactating women as it leads to various diseases and disabilities.

6.7 Intra-household discrimination in nutritional matters vis-a-vis girls and women will be sought to be ended through appropriate strategies. Widespread use of nutrition education would be made to address the issues of intra-household imbalances in nutrition and the special needs of pregnant and lactating women. Women's participation will also be ensured in the planning, superintendence and delivery of the system.

Drinking Water and Sanitation

6.8 Special attention will be given to the needs of

women in the provision of safe drinking water, sewage disposal, toilet facilities and sanitation within accessible reach of households, especially in rural areas and urban slums. Women's participation will be ensured in the planning, delivery and maintenance of such services.

Housing and Shelter

6.9 Women's perspectives will be included in the housing policies, planning of housing colonies and provision of shelter both in rural and urban areas. Special attention will be given for providing adequate and safe housing and accommodation for women including single women, heads of households, working women, students, apprentices and trainees.

Environment

6.10 Women will be involved and their perspectives reflected in the policies and programmes for environment, conservation and restoration. Considering the impact of environmental factors on their livelihoods, women's participation will be ensured in the conservation of the environment and control of environmental degradation. The vast majority of rural women still depend on the locally available non-commercial sources of energy such as animal dung, crop waste and fuel wood. In order to ensure the efficient use of these energy resources in an environmental friendly manner, the Policy will aim at promoting the programmes of non-conventional energy resources. Women will be involved in spreading the use of solar energy, biogas, smokeless chulahs and other rural application so as to have a visible impact of these measures in influencing eco system and in changing the life styles of rural women.

Science and Technology

6.11 Programmes will be strengthened to bring about a greater involvement of women in science and technology. These will include measures to motivate girls to take up science and technology for higher education and also ensure that development projects with scientific and technical inputs involve women fully. Efforts to develop a scientific temper and awareness will also be stepped up. Special measures would be taken for their training in areas where they have special skills like communication and information technology. Efforts to develop appropriate technologies suited to women's needs as well as to reduce their drudgery will be given a special focus too.

Women in Difficult Circumstances

6.12 In recognition of the diversity of women's situations and in acknowledgement of the needs of specially disadvantaged groups, measures and programmes will be undertaken to provide them with special assistance. These groups include women in extreme poverty, destitute women, women in conflict situations, women affected by natural calamities, women in less developed regions, the disabled widows, elderly women, single women in difficult circumstances, women heading households, those displaced from employment, migrants, women who are victims of marital violence, deserted women and prostitutes etc.

Violence against Women

7.1 All forms of violence against women, physical and mental, whether at domestic or societal levels, including those arising from customs, traditions or accepted practices shall be dealt with effectively with a view to eliminate its incidence. Institutions and mechanisms/schemes for assistance will be created and strengthened for prevention of such violence, including sexual harassment at work place and customs like dowry; for the rehabilitation of the victims of violence and for taking effective action against the perpetrators of such violence. A special emphasis will also be laid on programmes and measures to deal with trafficking in women and girls.

Rights of the Girl Child

8.1 All forms of discrimination against the girl child

and violation of her rights shall be eliminated by undertaking strong measures both preventive and punitive within and outside the family. These would relate specifically to strict enforcement of laws against prenatal sex selection and the practices of female foeticide, female infanticide, child marriage, child abuse and child prostitution etc. Removal of discrimination in the treatment of the girl child within the family and outside and projection of a positive image of the girl child will be actively fostered. There will be special emphasis on the needs of the girl child and earmarking of substantial investments in the areas relating to food and nutrition, health and education, and in vocational education. In implementing programmes for eliminating child labour, there will be a special focus on girl children.

Mass Media

9.1 Media will be used to portray images consistent with human dignity of girls and women. The Policy will specifically strive to remove demeaning, degrading and negative conventional stereotypical images of women and violence against women. Private sector partners and media networks will be involved at all levels to ensure equal access for women particularly in the area of information and communication technologies. The media would be encouraged to develop codes of conduct, professional guidelines and other self regulatory mechanisms to remove gender stereotypes and promote balanced portrayals of women and men.

Operational Strategies

Action Plans

10.1 All Central and State Ministries will draw up time bound Action Plans for translating the Policy into a set of concrete actions, through a participatory process of consultation with Centre/State Departments of Women and Child Development and National/State Commissions for Women. The Plans will specifically include the following:

i) Measurable goals to be achieved by 2010;

ii) Identification and commitment of resources;

iii) Responsibilities for implementation of action points;

iv) Structures and mechanisms to ensure efficient monitoring, review and gender impact assessment of action points and policies;

v) Introduction of a gender perspective in the budgeting process.

10.2 In order to support better planning and programme formulation and adequate allocation of resources, Gender Development Indices (GDI) will be developed by networking with specialised agencies. These could be analysed and studied in depth. Gender auditing and development of evaluation mechanisms will also be undertaken along side.

10.3 Collection of gender disaggregated data by all primary data collecting agencies of the Central and State Governments as well as Research and Academic Institutions in the public and private sectors will be undertaken. Data and information gaps in vital areas reflecting the status of women will be sought to be filled in by these immediately. All Ministers/Corporations/ Banks and financial institutions etc will be advised to collect, collate, disseminate and maintain/publish data related to programmes and benefits on a gender disaggregated basis. This will help in meaningful planning and evaluation of policies.

Institutional Mechanisms

11.1 Institutional mechanisms, to promote the advancement of women, which exist at the Central and State levels, will be strengthened. These will be through interventions as may be appropriate and will relate to, among others, provision of adequate resources training and advocacy skills to effectively influence macro-policies, legislation, programmes etc to achieve the empowerment of women.

11.2 National and State Councils will be formed to oversee the operationalisation of the Policy on a regular basis. The National Council will be headed by the Prime Minister and the State Councils by the Chief Ministers and will be broad in composition having representatives from the concerned Departments/Ministries, National and State Commissions for Women, Social Welfare Boards, representatives of Non-Government Organisations, Women's Organisations, Corporate Sector, Trade Unions, financing institutions, academics, experts and social activists etc. These bodies will review the progress made in implementing the Policy twice a year. The National Development Council will also be informed of the progress of the programme undertaken under the policy from time to time for advice and comments.

11.3 National and State Resource Centres on women will be established with mandates for collection and dissemination of information, undertaking research work, conducting surveys, implementing training and awareness generation programmes etc. These Centres will link up with Women's Studies Centres and other research and academic institutions through suitable information networking systems.

11.4 While institutions at the district level will be strengthened, at the grassroots, women will be helped by Government through its programmes to organise and strengthen into Self-Help Groups (SHGs) at the Anganwadi Village/Town level. The women's groups will be helped to institutionalise themselves into registered societies and to federate at the Panchayat/ Municipal level. These societies will bring about synergistic implementation of all the social and economic development programmes by drawing resources made available through Government and Non-Government channels, including banks and financial institutions and by establishing a close interface with the Panchayats/ Municipalities.

Resource Management

12.1 Availability of adequate financial, human and market resources to implement the Policy will be managed by concerned Departments, financial credit institutions and banks, private sector, civil society and other connected institutions. This process will include:

(a) Assessment of benefits flowing to women and resource allocation to the programmes relating to them through an exercise of gender budgeting. Appropriate changes in policies will be made to optimise benefits to women under these schemes.

(b) Adequate resource allocation to develop and promote the policy outlined earlier based on (a) above by concerned Departments.

(c) Developing synergy between personnel of Health, Rural Development, Education and Women & Child Development Department at field level and other village level functionaries.

(d) Meeting credit needs by banks and financial credit institutions through suitable policy initiatives and development of new institutions in coordination with the Department of Women & Child Development.

12.2 The strategy of Women's Component Plan adopted in the Ninth Plan of ensuring not less than 30% of benefits/funds flow to women from all Ministries and Departments will be implemented effectively so that the needs and interests of women and girls are addressed by all concerned sectors. The Department of Women and Child Development being the nodal Ministry will monitor and review the progress of the implementation of the Component Plan from time to time, in terms of both quality and quantity, in collaboration with the Planning Commission.

12.4 Efforts will be made to channelise private sector investments too, to support programmes and projects for advancement of women.

Legislation

13.1 The existing legislative structure will be reviewed and additional legislative measures taken by identified departments to implement the Policy. This will also involve a review of all existing laws including personal, customary and tribal laws, subordinate legislation, related rules as well as executive and administrative regulations to eliminate all gender discriminatory references. The process will be planned over a time period 2000-2003. The specific measures required would be evolved through a consultation process involving civil society, National Commission for Women and Department of Women and Child Development. In appropriate cases the consultation process would be widened to include other stakeholders too.

13.2 Effective implementation of legislation would be promoted by involving civil society and community. Appropriate changes in legislation will be undertaken, if necessary.

13.3 In addition, following other specific measures will be taken to implement the legislation effectively:

(a) Strict enforcement of all relevant legal provisions and speedy redressal of grievances will be ensured, with a special focus on violence and gender related atrocities;

(b) Measures to prevent and punish sexual harassment at the place of work, protection for women workers in the organised/unorganised sector and strict enforcement of relevant laws such as Equal Remuneration Act and Minimum Wages Act will be undertaken;

(c) Crimes against women, their incidence, prevention, investigation, detection and prosecution will be regularly reviewed at all

Crime Review fora and Conferences at the Central, State and District levels. Recognised local, voluntary organisations will be authorised to lodge complaints and facilitate registration, investigations and legal proceedings related to violence and atrocities against girls and women;

(d) Women's Cells in Police Stations, Women Police Stations, Family Courts, Mahila Courts, Counselling Centres, Legal Aid Centres and Nyaya Panchayats will be strengthened and expanded to eliminate violence and atrocities against women;

(e) Widespread dissemination of information on all aspects of legal rights, human rights and other entitlements of women, through specially designed legal literacy programmes and rights information programmes will be done.

Gender Sensitisation

14.2 Training of personnel of executive, legislative and judicial wings of the State, with a special focus on policy and programme framers, implementation and development agencies, law enforcement machinery and the judiciary, as well as non-governmental organisations will be undertaken. Other measures will include:

a) Promoting societal awareness to gender issues and women's human right;

b) Review of curriculum and educational materials to include gender education and human rights issues;

(c) Removal of all references derogatory to the dignity of women from all public documents and legal instruments;

(f) Use of different forms of mass media to communicate social messages relating to women's equality and empowerment.

Panchayati Raj Institutions

5.1 The 73rd and 74th Amendments (1993) to the Indian Constitution have served as a breakthrough towards ensuring equal access and increased participation in political power structure for women. The PRIs will play a central role in the process of enhancing women's participation in public life. The PRIs and the local self governments will be actively involved in the implementation and execution of the National Policy for Women at the grassroots level.

Partnership with the Voluntary Sector Organisations

6.1 The involvement of voluntary organisations, associations, federations, trade unions, non-governmental organisations, women's organisations, as well as institutions dealing with education, training and research will be ensured in the formulation, implementation, monitoring and review of all policies and programmes affecting women. Towards this end, they will be provided with appropriate support related to resources and capacity building and facilitated to participate actively in the process of the empowerment of women.

International Cooperation

17.1 The Policy will aim at implementation of international obligations/commitments in all sectors on empowerment of women such as the Convention on the Elimination of All Forms of Discrimination against Women (CEDAW), Convention on the Rights of the Child (CRC), International Conference on Population and Development (ICPD+5) and other such instruments. International, regional and sub-regional cooperation towards the empowerment of women will continue to be encouraged through sharing of experiences, exchange of ideas and technology, networking with institutions and organisations and through bilateral and multi-lateral partnerships.

■■■

INDEX

■■■